Henriette Mandl

Henriette Mandl

Vienna
Downtown Walking Tours

Ueberreuter

Picture credits

Bildarchiv der Österreichischen Nationalbibliothek: I/14, II/31,
III/64, III/67, III/70, III/77, III/82, III/84, IV/105, V/157,
VI/171, VI/195
Bundesdenkmalamt Wien: I/19, I/22, II/34, II/54, IV/114,
V/133, V/150, VI/180, VI/182, VI/185
Lotte Hendrich-Hassmann: II/49, III/89, IV/97, IV/122,
V/135, V/144, VI/176
Peter Hassmann: I/9
Franz Hubmann: II/52, II/57, III/75
Heinz Fischer: III/61
Nö. Landesregierung: V/148
Fremdenverkehrsstelle der Stadt Wien (Walden): VI/174
Fotostudio Fasching: II/41
Fremdenverkehrsverband Wien: V/155

Deutsche Bibliothek Cataloguing in Publication Data

Mandl, Henriette:
Vienna downtown walking tours /
Henriette Mandl. – Wien : Ueberreuter, 1987.
Dt. Ausg. u. d. T.: Mandl, Henriette:
Wiener Altstadt-Spaziergänge
ISBN 3-8000-3242-2

AU 57/1
All rights reserved
Jacket Layout by Atelier Graupner & Partners, Munich
© 1987 by Verlag Carl Ueberreuter, Vienna
Produced by Carl Ueberreuter Druckerei Ges. m. b. H.,
2100 Korneuburg
Printed in Austria

INTRODUCTION

When in a foreign city, do you enjoy little excursions on your own, on foot and "far from the madding crowd"? I do—and in the hope of finding similarly inclined fellow-explorers I have collected these legends, stories and gossip. I used to roam the Inner City of Vienna with visitors from abroad and they loved getting to know hidden treasures, to look at what superficially seems to be a very ordinary, unexciting building and to suddenly see it in quite a different light: clothed in romance, awe-inspiring through its historic significance or conjuring up some delightful episode, full of fun and laughter.

"Where is all this written down?" they would ask. The answer so far was "Nowhere, at least not in English". Some of it is taken straight from the old chronicles, some has come down to us by word of mouth through the ages and then, of course, some of it has been collected in books, magazines and newspapers—but most of it is in German, occasionally even in Viennese dialect. So I have compiled what seemed to me worth passing on to people interested in the past and present "inner" life of this city. For though some of the stories may not be true, their very falseness gives a clue to the Viennese character and mirrors the way of life in this city more truly than many a bald fact or proven theory.

Ideally this should be your companion on many a pleasant stroll through little narrow streets, it should lead you away from the beaten tourist track and open up vistas unknown and unsuspected in the busy life of a large metropolis—and finally it should become a welcome souvenir to re-read and bring back happy memories once you are back home again.

Just one word of caution: Vienna is a living city—things change. It is therefore possible that you will find that a description of some house no longer applies or the given opening hours are no longer valid. I can only hope this will not seriously impair your enjoyment of the tours.

Vienna, Spring 1987   Henriette Mandl

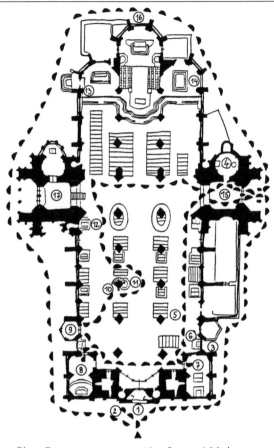

1. Giant Gate
2. Standard Measurements
3. Neidhart's Tomb
4. St. Catherine's Chapel
5. Madonna with the
   Protective Cloak
6. Maria-Pötsch-Altar
7. Chapel of St. Eligius
8. Tirna Chapel
9. Rudolph's Epitaph and
   St. Coloman's Stone
10. Servants' Madonna
11. Pulpit
12. Organ Base
13. Rudolph's Tombstone
14. Frederick's Tomb
15. South Tower (Old Steve)
16. Our Lord of the
    Toothache
17. North Tower

FIRST TOUR

St. Stephen's Cathedral

St. Stephen's Cathedral

If you are a stranger to Vienna and wondering where best to begin exploring the city, the obvious starting point is St. Stephen's Cathedral. It is easily accessible either by bus or by subway, but should you be in the mood for walking, it is not all that far from the Opera. It is therefore from this point that most of the tours will start. Let us now take the Cathedral itself as the first one.

For more than 800 years St. Stephen's has shared the varied destiny of this city. Today it is considered the heart of Vienna, its centre. This was, however, not always so, for when the church was built in 1137, it was outside the town wall and not incorporated until the first city expansion 18 years later.

The Viennese feel an inexplicable tenderness for this ancient landmark, an attachment which became very evident during the last days of the Second World War. The Russians already held the Inner City, while the Germans had withdrawn to the Danube Canal where they were desparately trying to hold their positions. In the ensuing battle, St. Stephen's came directly into their firing line and the roof of the Cathedral caught fire. Word went from mouth to mouth that St. Stephen's was burning and the Viennese came from all over the city to help extinguish the flames. When this was accomplished, they helped extricate every piece of broken vaulting or statuary from the ashes and rubble in order to ensure the possibility of its future reconstruction.

The Romanesque main entrance is called "Das Riesentor" (the Giant Gate). The name, however, does not refer to its size. In 1443, when the foundations of the North Tower were being excavated, workmen found a giant bone, presumably belonging to a mammoth. This enormous fossil was hung on display above the main entrance until the 18th century. Frederick III, who had a mania for marking everything he could lay his hands on with the cryptic initials AEIOU, left their message on this bone. The letters have been interpreted to mean Austria

The Giant Gate of St. Stephen's

erit in orbe ultimo (Austria will exist forever), or Austriae est imperare omni universo (The entire universe is subjugated by Austria).

Before moving closer, look up and slightly to the left, quite high, you will see a niche in which a man is sitting. He is generally referred to as the "man with a thorn", because with one leg resting on his other knee he reminds one of the antique statue of the thorn-removing boy. It still remains a mystery what this figure signifies; the generally accepted interpretation is that it represents the temporal judge as opposed to Christ, the Divine Judge, who sits above the main entrance.

To the left of the portal there is a faint circle on the wall. The popular belief is that it was the standard size of a loaf of bread. Anyone suspecting a baker of cheating could check the size of the loaf he had bought against the circle on the church wall. If the baker was found guilty of selling undersize bread, he was put in a wooden cage and ducked in the Danube. But there is also an old legend connected with this circle.

In a village in Lower Austria there once lived a wicked woman. Her husband, a well-to-do miller, died young and she was not entirely innocent of his death. Once she inherited the mill, she grew meaner and more hard-hearted, for even though she was now rich, she left her brother and his family to starve.

One day a beggar appeared at her door, imploring her to give him just a crust of stale bread, but she sent him away empty-handed. Before leaving he cursed her, saying: "Your bread shall be as hard as your heart is!"

This curse soon proved to be no empty threat. When the woman went to her kitchen, she found the bread had turned to stone, her larder was bare and her coffers were empty. She was beset by contrition and, having heard of miracles which had been wrought at St. Stephen's in Vienna, she journeyed to the city and finally arrived at the Cathedral, where she confessed her sin to a priest. The good man would not give her absolution, but told her she might take up her place outside the main gate where repenting sinners stood until they were forgiven.

Many a day she stood there in all kinds of weather until one day she noticed the faint circle against the wall which looked just like the loaf of bread that had turned to stone. She took this to be a sign of her forgiveness and hurried to tell the priest, who then absolved her.

Just underneath the breadloaf are two iron bars, one a little longer than the other. These are "the little ell" and "the big ell". The first measures 0.78 meters ($30^1/_2$ inches), while the second, a measurement used in the building trade, is 0.89 meters (35 inches). They were regarded as standard measurements and both bricks and cloths were brought here in case of doubt.

On the right side of the main gate you will see 'O5' scratched into the wall's surface. This was the symbol of the Austrian Resistance Movement or, to be more exact, the symbol for the Provisory Austrian National Committee which took up contact with the governments of the approaching armies in March 1945, at which time this sign appeared on the wall of St. Stephen's.

Let us walk on to the right and turn the corner. A few steps further on there is a recess, and behind an iron bar stands a tomb with a very much damaged recumbent figure. It is supposed to be Neidhart Fuchs, jester and poet at the Court of Otto the Joyous. At one time a coat-of-arms depicting a fox was still visible. Some claim that this tomb is the last resting place of the minnesinger Neidhart von Reuenthal (1180–1240). Be that as it may, the poems attributed to Fuchs at a later date certainly owe much of their satirical realism to Reuenthal, who was the first to break with the romantic troubadour tradition in favour of a cruder, more realistic and erotic language.

But let us return to Neidhart Fuchs. He seems to have been a jolly fellow, who wrote several amusing stories in verse. As it happens, most of them made fun of the peasants and he was therefore known as "the peasants' enemy".

One of these stories goes as follows: In those days it was the custom that whoever found the first violet in the Vienna Woods put his hat over it and ran to town to tell the Court the good news. The Duke and all his retainers immediately set forth with music and rejoicing to view this first messenger of spring. Once it was Neidhart's good fortune to discover the first violet and, as required, he put his hat over it and hurried to town.

While he was gone some peasants came by, saw and recognised Neidhart's hat and thought this an excellent opportunity to repay him for many a quip he had made at their expense.

When the Court arrived in the woods, the poet proudly

went to lift his hat. To his horror there was no violet beneath it. I had better leave it to your imagination what he found there. Let it suffice to say that it certainly did not smell sweet!

Next to Neidhart's tomb there used to be an entrance to the church which, however, has not been used for years. It goes by the name of 'Singertor'–whether on account of the singer's tomb beside it or because it faces in the direction of Singerstrasse is unclear. In the old days the main entrance was opened only on special occasions, whereas the side entrances were used regularly. This one was the door used by the men, for St. Stephen's–like most European churches during the Middle Ages and some country churches to this day–had the women all segregated on one side of the nave, while the men were on the other. This being the men's entrance it features male saints only.

The Singertor was also known as the Rendezvous-Door, because it was a favourite meeting-place for lovers in days gone by.

Before leaving, look up at the grotesque gargoyles–water spouts–that are making faces at you from above.

A little further on we come upon a larger entrance, known as the Primglöckleintor, named after the bell housed above it, which rang for prayer at 6 a.m. This portal is directly under the large South Tower and through it we enter the Cathedral. It is worth glancing at the photographs to the left which give some clue to the ravages St. Stephen's suffered at the end of World War II.

Inside we are steeped in the twilight of the past. Immediately to your right is a chapel closed off by a wrought-iron gate; it is dedicated to St. Catherine and contains a beautiful Gothic baptismal font dated 1481. The lid of this font has a strange history. For decades, possibly centuries, it was used as a sounding board over the pulpit in the nave. I remember it well, for that was where it hung in my childhood. After it fell during the holocaust of 1945, one of the art historians from the University who was active in helping salvage everything possible from the rubble, noticed its strange dimensions. He measured and re-measured it, noted the fact that it showed the seven sacraments and at the very top the baptism of Christ and finally made the fantastic discovery that it was, in fact, the cover of the font in St. Catherine's Chapel.

Walking into the main body of the church, we turn left into the aisle. When we reach the last pillar on the right, there, quite far up, is a slender statue of Our Lady holding the Christ Child. Within the folds of her cloak a multitude of people are seeking shelter. She is a "Madonna with the Protective Cloak". This statue was donated by Dorothea, widow of Konrad Vorlauf, the Mayor of Vienna, who was executed by Duke Leopold in 1408 (see p. 169). Kneeling on the left, his hat in front of him, is Vorlauf himself, with his two patron saints and angels behind him. On the other side, there is Dorothea his wife–his fifth wife, as a matter of fact–with her two daughters and again the heads of angels above them. At the Virgin's feet is Vorlauf's coat-of-arms: a rampant horse.

Let us continue to where a great many candles are burning before an altar. It is a Madonna from Pötsch (now Pecs) in Hungary, that is venerated here. This picture became famous in the 17th century when many witnesses spread the story that real tears poured down the cheeks of the Virgin. The moisture on the painting was even examined by scholars and found to have the same consistency as human tears. It was brought to Vienna and at one time graced the High Altar. People pray to this particular miraculous image to entreat a cure for the sick.

To the right of the altar, on the wall there is a memorial for one Martin Keckmann and though it is usually rather dark at this end of the church, you may just be able to discern a kneeling man at the front of the relief and next to him a shaggy little dog. Keep this dog in mind, you will shortly meet his brother.

At the very end of the aisle to the left, there is a door to a chapel that is only open for prayer in the evening between 7 and 10 p.m. It is consecrated to St. Eligius, who was the patron saint of the Guild of Goldsmiths. It

The little dog on the Keckmann memorial

houses one of the most lovely statues of the Virgin Mary. It came from the convent of "The Gates of Heaven" (Himmelpfortkloster), where it was known as "Die Hausmuttergottes", so to speak their own special Mother of God. She is supposed to have protected the convent, especially in times when the plague ravaged the City. In 1679, for instance, the convent did not have a single case among its inmates. The statue also goes by the name of "Himmelspförtnerin" (The Portress at the Gates of Heaven, for which see p. 46).

Coming out of this chapel, we traverse the entire width of the Cathedral. Pause a moment in the centre aisle and let the grandeur of its Gothic splendour sink in.

To the far left there is also a chapel, the Tirna or Holy Cross Chapel, where Prince Eugene of Savoy is buried. It is usually closed and thus the first impression is of the lovely wrought-iron gate, reminiscent of the park entrances to Eugene's Belvedere Palace. Peering through it, you can see the very plain tombstone covering the burial vault on the floor. Behind the pillar to the left, however, there is a more elaborate memorial, which is not visible from where you are standing.

Prince Eugene, of legendary fame even in his lifetime, was given a sumptuous state funeral. The Emperor, Charles VI, paid for it and obviously felt that it was time the heirs took over with regard to erecting a memorial. Though Prince Eugene had by no means died a poor man–he had left over a million Guilders to his grand-niece Anna Victoria–this lady had no intention of doing her duty by her illustrious relative, and the Viennese are supposed to have been rather disgusted at her behaviour. The lady was, in general, not worthy of her inheritance–the palaces, famous library and art collection were all sold post-haste.

And it was finally, eighteen years after the Prince's death, another relative, the wife of his nephew, who gave instructions for the erection of the memorial.

Due to construction work in connection with the subway, the burial vault of Prince Eugene had to be opened in 1974. It was found to contain three coffins and an urn destined to contain a heart. Two of the coffins were easily identified by their inscriptions. They hold the remains of the Prince's nephew and his wife. The third coffin, however, bears no inscription at all and the only clue to its occupant is the heart urn on top of it. This urn bears the following words: "Heart of His Serene Highness Eugene Francis, Prince of Savoy, who died in Vienna on April 21, 1736."

This was a surprise and led to various speculations. It has always been assumed that Prince Eugene's heart was taken to Torino, where it is supposedly buried. King Victor Amadeus had had a church built to commemorate Prince Eugene's liberation of the city in 1706 and it was to be the burial site for the House of Savoy. If the heart urn does indeed contain the heart, what is it doing in Vienna? Was it only used to convey the heart to Torino, where another urn was awaiting it and after the heart had been transferred, was the empty urn returned to Vienna? In that case why the elaborate inscription? Or is the Italian theory correct, that the heart is no longer in Torino at all, but was secretly smuggled back to Vienna when, at the end of the 18th century, Torino was in danger of being occupied by the French–and as they had no reason to love the Prince, who had defeated them in many a battle–it was feared they would desecrate his tomb.

Thus the situation at present is still unclarified. So far no second heart urn has been found in Torino and we still do not know what the urn in St. Stephen's contains. Even if the Vienna urn holds the Prince's heart, this still does not answer the questions: was it never sent to Torino? Or, if it was, when was it returned and why?

Above the altar in this chapel there is a large crucifix. The figure on it happens to have a beard of real hair, which gave rise to the legend that it grows and has to be trimmed every Good Friday. The chapel, therefore, is also known as the Chapel of Our Lord's Hairgrowth.

Turning your back on the chapel, there is an altar to your left and right next to it a small statue of St. Jude Thaddeus. He is a very recent addition and, as such, is not of great interest. But he always puts me in mind of Josef Weinheber's poem: "Before and after", which in translation reads something like this:

> O, St. Thaddeus help me, I pray!
> I'll bring you a candle another day.
> You've helped me, I thank you,
> I gather that now
> You don't need a candle anyhow?

Beside the statue is the porch of the north-west entrance, at one time the women's entrance. The porch area is now being used as a shop for candles, postcards and booklets on the Cathedral. Let us go in here.

16

On the right-hand wall you can see some cryptic signs. For hundreds of years men wondered what they could mean and it was not until the middle of the 18th century that it was decyphered as: "Hic est sepultus Dei gratia dux Rudolphus Fundator" (Here, by the grace of God, Duke Rudolph the Founder lies buried). The writing, it is thought, was invented by Rudolph himself and bears a resemblance to the signs used by the masons' lodges of his time. But Rudolph is not buried behind this wall at all. Nor, for that matter, is he buried in the sumptuous tomb to the left of the Wiener Neustädter altar, though his effigy and that of his wife Catherine, crown this monument. His resting place is in the catacombs with so many of his peers.

This Rudolph is a fascinating figure in Austrian history. He began his reign at the age of nineteen and died when he was only twenty-six. But in the short space of seven years he immortalized himself by laying the foundations, not only of the Gothic part of the Cathedral, but also of the Vienna University (see p. 87). In addition, he forged a document, the so-called "privilegium maius", in which the Austrian Dukes are ranked with the German electors and may claim the title of Archdukes. The Emperor Charles IV rejected this document for the fake it was and Rudolph had to relinquish his self-imposed title of Archduke. Nevertheless, this was by no means the end of the matter, for almost a hundred years later another Habsburg was to confirm the title as genuine.

Standing in the porch, to the right of the door is a statue of Rudolph holding a model of St. Stephen's. By the way, one of the first portraits to be painted since antiquity is that of Rudolph. This painting can be seen at the Dom- and Diözesanmuseum at Stephansplatz No. 6, which also possesses his brocade winding-sheet. Rudolph died in Milan and was transported to Vienna, sewn into a cowhide to preserve the body.

It was also Rudolph who put St. Coloman's stone in the porch. You are hardly likely to find this ancient relic because it is hidden by the usually open glass door. But if you ask the sales lady's permission, she will no doubt let you shut the door for a few seconds. There, in the wall behind it, is a black stone which has become hollowed and whitened by the hands of many pious pilgrims over the ages.

Now practically invisible, the inscription reads: "This is the stone on to which the blood of the Holy Martyr Coloman flowed when his shins were sawn to pieces. The noble Lord Rudolph IV, Duke of Austria, put it here."

Coloman's story is as follows: He was an Irishman of royal descent who left his country to go on a pilgrimage to the Holy Land. While passing through Austria, he was taken for a spy, imprisoned and found guilty because he had parchments on him in a foreign language. He was put to horrible tortures, as the above inscription indicates, and though he tried to prove his innocence by signs, this merely infuriated his torturers even more. Finally, the poor man gave up the ghost. But no sooner was he dead and buried than miracles started to happen. The loveliest flowers sprouted on his grave and when the Danube flooded the entire area the following year, his place of burial alone was left unharmed.

Hearing of these strange signs, Margrave Henry had Coloman's remains exhumed, intending to give them decent burial, only to find that the body was untouched by decay as if the deceased had only just breathed his last. On October 13, 1014, Coloman was transferred to a tomb at the monastery of Melk.

Back to the main body of the church and this time we walk to the third column at the base of which a graceful, smiling statue of Virgin and Child stands. This is the "Dienstbotenmadonna" (the Servants' Madonna) and again a legend is connected with it.

Many years ago there lived a rich countess in Vienna, who spent much time going to church and praying. In fact, she even had a private chapel in her own home. However, when she wasn't on her knees, she was known to be a veritable devil and was greatly feared by her servants. Among these, there was a young girl, an orphan, who had nowhere else to go. This girl had a particularly

The Servants' Madonna

hard time as the Countess would scold her and find fault with her continually.

One day the Countess discovered that a precious pearl necklace had disappeared from her jewelry box; without hesitation she accused the poor girl of having stolen it, claiming she was the only one who had had access to the jewels.

The police were called and the miserable servant girl,

despite her protestations of innocence, was on the point of the being arrested. In her dire need, she ran into the chapel and threw herself on her knees before the statue of the Virgin Mary, praying: "Help me, blessed Virgin!" The Countess had followed her, and new sneered: "That Madonna is mine, she was made for me and she is not likely to listen to a mere servant". "Oh, Mary, Mother of God", cried the poor girl desperately, clinging to the base of the statue, "say it isn't true, show me that you *do* listen do a servant's prayer and prove me innocence in the face of these unjust accusations."

The police officer who had witnessed this whole scene, now began to wonder. He ordered a search to be made and, lo and behold, before long the pearls were found among the belongings of one of the stable boys. When confronted, he admitted to the theft and the girl was set free.

The rich Countess, however, was displeased with the statue for having wrought a miracle for a servant and no longer wanted it in her chapel. She therefore donated it to St. Stephen's Cathedral.

Very soon the story of the servant girl's miraculous salvation spread all over the city and this statue aquired the reputation of being the special protectress of servants, which it has remained to this day.

This same third column, though, is the site of yet another wonder: the pulpit. Built by the master builder Anton Pilgram, it is the epitome of late Gothic sculpture. The four Fathers of the Church, Gregory, Jerome, Augustine and Ambrose, with those incredibly expressive faces, are looking down at you. But let me draw your attention to "all kinds of vermin", toads and lizards, crawling up the banisters. At the top there is a little shaggy dog, a symbol of vigilance, who keeps them at bay. Here, too, the interpretations vary. One claims that these are all creatures of darkness, trying to intercept the Word of God; another is of the opinion that the toads are creatures of darkness, while lizards love the light and there is a battle going on between them. Just a word more about the little dog: he—or his twin brother—can be seen in the Keckmann

Selfportrait of Master Anton Pilgram

memorial on the wall beside the Maria Pötsch altar. This has prompted art historians to attribute the memorial to Master Anton Pilgram. Moreover, a likeness has been discovered in the faces of the Pilgram self-portrait–"the man looking out of the window"–underneath the pulpit and St. Martin, the bishop celebrating mass on the plaque.

A little further east on the left-hand wall there is a magnificent organ pedestal–again ending in a self-portrait of Master Pilgram. The organ pedestal was a daring piece of work. His fellow masons scoffed at him and warned him that the delicate structure would never hold the organ that was to stand on it. Pilgram got angry and answered them: "Well, if it won't hold the organ, than *I* will!" Therefore, in his self-portrait below it, he seems to be bearing the load of the entire pedestal on his back.

Usually the altars in the chancel are cordoned off and you may only enter with a guide. But if you go forward as far as possible you can see the magnificent carved wooden altar at the end of the left aisle, the Wiener Neustädter altar. Perhaps you are in luck and a mass is about to be celebrated or has just ended, enabling you to take a closer look. If so, don't fail to go to the left where the large sarcophagus of Rudolph the Founder stands. Unfortunately, it is rather too high and so the splendid recumbent figures of Rudolph and his wife Katherina can hardly be seen (see p. 17).

Now walk all the way to the right aisle and take up your position at the barrier, from where you can just see the tomb of Frederick III at the far end.

This tomb is one of the sights of the Cathedral. The Emperor had summoned the famous Flemish sculptor Niclas Gerhaert van Leyden to Austria to build this monument. The sculptor started work in 1467, but when Frederick died in 1493, only the lid of the tomb had been finished. So Frederick was meanwhile buried in the Princes' Vault and later, after completion of the tomb in 1513, he was ceremoniously transferred to it.

However, as the Emperor had died at Linz and his tomb was not ready for another twenty years, there was a persistent rumour that he was never buried in it at all. On account of this rumour, a scientific experiment took place on March 12, 1969, which is probably unique of its kind. One of the slabs depicting coats-of-arms on the tomb was carefully removed, and a probe infiltrated into the interior burial chamber. This probe had a lighted reflecting mirror at its end. The reflector showed a piece of the cloth of red and gold material which, according to the chronicles, had been used as a shroud for the Emperor. This proved that Frederick did, finally, come to rest in his own tomb.

We now leave through the south door, the way we came in, and cross to the other side of the street in order to get a better view of our next object: the large South Tower. St. Stephen's Tower is the heart of Vienna and every Viennese has a weak spot for this most famous landmark. I well remember when, in 1954, the news spread that the high tower of St. Stephen's, lovingly referred to as "der alte Steffel" (old Steve), was to be put in scaffolding for major repairs which were to last twelve years. On the night before the scaffolding was to be put up, the tower was floodlit and thousands of people thronged the streets around the Cathedral "to see Old Steve in his glory for the last time". It was a moving moment and, caught tightly in the midst of the throng, I marvelled at the sentimental attachment so many citizens feel for a mere stone tower.

The tower has, time and again, tempted daredevils to climb it. The last of them was a gardener's apprentice, one Gabriel Satzberger, who tried his luck in 1658 on the occasion of the Emperor's triumphal entry into Vienna. He wanted to greet his monarch by waving a flag from the top of the tower. Unfortunately, the procession was delayed and darkness fell before he could descend. Later no one was able to come to his aid and the poor man was forced to spend the night clinging to the tower in fear of his life. When the sun rose and people finally came to his rescue, his hair had turned completely white.

You, too, may wish to climb the tower, but it is advisable to use the inside winding staircase which takes you up to the chamber where the fire-guards at one time held their vigil. In order to help them pass the time, there is supposed to have been a bowling alley up there, to which the warden used to invite his cronies for a game. Once there was a wild fellow among them who boasted of always being able to get "all nine". His companions, even the warden himself, had long since retired for the night and still this fellow went on bowling. Suddenly, a spindly man, dressed all in grey, stood at his side and whispered: "Stop your game. It is late and there's the bell ringing for some poor soul about to die!" However, the fellow refused to listen, and even invited the stranger to join him in a game. After a further warning had been disregarded, the newcomer grew angry and took up the challenge. The boaster went to set up the pins, but while doing so, he threw one of them out of the window. At that moment the haggard little man turned into a huge skeleton holding an hour-glass and called out in a terrible voice: "I'll get all nine, even if there are only eight pins there!" Then with great force he threw the ball. The eight pins went down but so did the wicked bowler. Death had felled him like a ninepin.

They say, that he haunts the tower at midnight, looking for the ninth pin and will not be redeemed until he finds it.

Walking on around the church you finally reach a suffering Christ with a crown of thorns on a pedestal. This is the famous "Zahnwehherrgott" (Our Lord of the Toothache). The name may seem strange to you, but it is due to the following legend: The statue used to stand in the cemetery surrounding the Cathedral and people would decorate it with flowers. It so happened that one day an old woman had put a wreath of them over the statue's head. The wreath had slipped a little to one side and looked slightly ridiculous.

Towards dawn next morning three lads, who had been drinking most of the night, passed by. They were in very high spirits and one of them saw the statue with its wreath. He burst out laughing: "Look, just look," he spluttered, "Our Lord has got a toothache!" His two companions thought this extremely funny and the three of them went into such paroxysms of laughter that the people in the neighbouring houses opened their shutters and angrily told them to be quiet and let decent folk get their sleep.

The young men, still giggling uncontrollably, made their way home. But hardly had they gone to bed than they were beset by a terrible toothache. Whatever they tried, hot poultices, soothing potions or powders, nothing helped. Driven almost mad with the pain, one of them ran to a barber (it was the barbers who extracted teeth in those days). But the man could find nothing wrong and short of extracting all the boy's teeth, he could see no way of alleviating his pain. It was then that it began to dawn on the sufferer that this was a punishment for his blasphemy. As fast as his legs would carry him, he ran to

"Zahnwehherrgott" (Our Lord of the Toothache)

the cemetery and threw himself on his knees before the statue of Christ in deep contrition. Almost immediately the toothache began to recede and when he looked up in gratitude, he noticed that his two companions were there beside him–both obviously for the very same reason. After they had made a vow never to blaspheme again, the toothache subsided and ashamed, but grateful, they crept home.

Proceeding round the church the North Tower, or Eagle Tower as it is sometimes called, comes into view. Actually it is merely the rudiments of a tower. Originally Master Hans Puchsbaum had intended it as a rival for the South Tower, Old Steve, but in 1511 work on it stopped and apart from the Renaissance top added later, it was never taken up again. Naturally a phenomenon like that was ideal ground for the growth of a legend. And here it is:

Hans Puchsbaum was working as a mason under Master Mason Prachatitz and he happened to be in love with his master's daughter Maria. But Prachatitz would not hear of their marrying and told the young man that a union with his daughter was only possible if he were to complete the newly begun North Tower at the same time as he, Prachatitz, finished the almost completed South Tower. As this was not humanly possible, Puchsbaum fell into a depression, seeing every possibility of ever attaining his beloved vanish.

One day while he was on the platform of the scaffolding, a man appeared at his side and asked him the cause of his sadness. Puchsbaum told him of Master Prachatitz' impossible demand. The stranger became very interested and after they had talked for a while, he offered to help the young mason in his plight. "All you need to promise is, that you will never mention the name of God or any of his saints while working on the tower and I guarantee that you will finish it at the same time as Prachatitz completes his South Tower." Puchsbaum gladly agreed to this seemingly simple request and, sure enough, from that day on the construction proceeded with uncanny speed.

While at work one fine day, Puchsbaum happened to look down to the cemetery below and there he saw his sweetheart Maria. Without thinking, he called out to her "Maria!" But that was his undoing as it is the name of the Blessed Virgin. The devil–for it had been he who had tempted Puchsbaum–appeared on the tower and pushed the young man off. No trace of his body was ever found. But no one dared to work on the tower after that.

Facts, of course, do not correspond to legends. Prachatitz finished the South Tower in 1433 after it had been under construction for 74 years. Puchsbaum was nominated Master Mason of St. Stephen's in 1446 when he was 56 years old and then the North Tower was begun according to his design. He died in 1454.

Let us walk closer to the church again and next to the pulpit protruding, you will see the entrance to the catacombs (though nowadays you go down to them from inside the Cathedral).

It was from here that Mozart set out on his last journey on December 6, 1791. People have often been shocked at the fact that nobody really knows exactly where he is buried in the cemetery of St. Marx. Was it the weather or fear of contagion–for the cause of his death was not clearly known–that prevented the small gathering of his friends from following the coffin? The film "Amadeus" also stresses the grim aspects of this funeral, which, however, is probably historically close to the truth. For in 1784, Emperor Joseph II decreed that all sumptuous and expensive funerals were to be stopped. Henceforth the dead were to be wrapped in sackcloth winding sheets only and taken to mass graves in coffins that opened at one end. The body was thus tipped into the pit and the coffin could be used again. A most enlightened idea, but one that found little love among the populace and had to be repealed shortly. Nevertheless, we know that the poorer classes availed themselves of this kind of burial for years and as Mozart on the one hand died practically a pauper and on the other within seven years of the imperial decree, it is more than likely that this was the kind of burial he received.

Right under the North Tower is the Adlertor (Eagle Entrance). On the left pillar of the central doorway there is a strange iron handle, somewhat reminiscent of a huge empty spool. It is the old sanctuary handle. Whoever clasped this ring could not be handed over to the jurisdiction of the lay courts unless his crime was such that not even the church could absolve him of it.

And the last of the curiosities of St. Stephen's is a niche in the wall west of the so-called Eagle Gate. It is slightly below and to the left of a statue of the suffering Christ and is covered by a metal grating. At one time there were three stone images, remnants of some heathen altar, behind it. These went by the name of "Tatermandeln". The Viennese, always imaginative in their appelations, christened them "Luziferl, Spirifankerl and Springinkerl". They were presumed to be mischievous spirits which were finally caught and put into this cage from where there was no escape–so it was thought.

They are no longer there, so at some time they must have eluded their gaolers and are afoot in Vienna once more. There is no doubt about it, if anything unpleasant happens to you while you are in this city, they are the ones to blame!

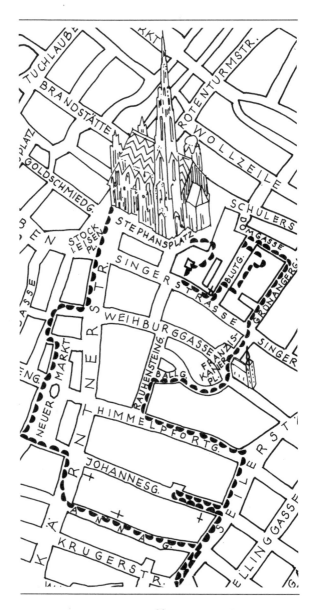

SECOND TOUR

Das Deutsche Haus
Singerstrasse
Blutgasse
Domgasse
Grünangergasse
Franziskanerplatz
Ballgasse
Rauhensteingasse
Himmelpfortgasse
Seilerstätte
Johannesgasse
Annagasse
Kärntner Strasse
Neuer Markt
Kärntner Durchgang

Das Deutsche Haus

At the back of St. Stephen's Cathedral, almost opposite
Our Lord of the Toothache, is "Das Deutsche Haus" (literally the German House). In spite of its name, it has
nothing to do with Germany, but is called after the Teutonic Knights, a religious Order of Hospitalers founded
during the Crusades, in which these knights cared for
sick pilgrims and wounded crusaders. In 1205, the
Church donated this complex of buildings to the Order,
it comprised living quarters for its members, as well as a
barn, domestic offices and the adjoining chapel.

But we are still standing on Stephansplatz. Towards the
right-hand corner there is a small door, Stephansplatz
No. 4 and this is where we will enter. Sometimes the
door is locked, in which case the courts which lie behind
it can be entered from Singerstrasse No. 7. Once inside
the first court, we turn right and come to an archway,
leading to a second, smaller court. Under the archway
you will find the names of many a famous musician listed
either among those who are honorary members of the
Mozart Society or bearers of the Mozart medal, for the
house is closely connected with this composer. It was
here that he lived while in the services of Archbishop
Count Colloredo from March 16 to May 2, 1781. Poor
Mozart, he wasn't very happy here. The Archbishop was
extremely rude to the young musician, only twenty-five
at the time, but already very famous. He did not care to
be treated like a mere servant and after a heated argument with his employer Mozart left the Archbishop's services.

The enchanting little courtyard is graced by an unexpected statue of St. Catherine and if you look up, you
will be surprised to find St. Stephen's spire looking down
at you over the rooftop. The tranquillity of the spot is liable to make us forget how close we are to the centre of
town.

The glass door on the other side leads into a vestibule.
To the left, there is a plaque which tells of Mozart's
short stay and next to it an impressive staircase leading

The windows of Mozart's first quarters in Vienna

up to the treasury of the Teutonic Order which, if you can spare the time, is worth a visit. The brotherhood was certainly not a poor one, for, on initiation, its members had to vow a lifetime of chastity, celibacy and poverty, as well as obedience. As most of them came from the aristocracy and had to relinquish their worldly goods, the Order became very prosperous.

To the left of the large entrance, which takes us out to the street, a door opens on to the chapel. And what a beauty it is: the Gothic vaulting, the walls bearing the coats-of-arms of the knights of past ages. A lovely wooden carved altar from Malines serves as a reminder that this distant town was once part of the Habsburg possessions. There are also several rather ornate tombstones which somehow do not quite tally with the alleged poverty of their owners. For lovers of the Gregorian chant, it might be of interest to know that this is sung at evening mass here on Sundays and feast days.

These Teutonic Knights must have been a striking sight clad in their white uniforms, black jackboots and white cloaks with a black cross, carrying a wide-brimmed, feather-trimmed hat.

But let us leave the knights and go out through the large doorway which brings us on to Singerstrasse.

Singerstrasse

This is one of the oldest streets in Vienna. It is mentioned as early as 1314 as Sunigerstrasse, for it was the weavers and dyers from the town of Sünchingen, near Regensburg, who populated this region. By 1550, we hear of it being called Singerstrasse.

Turning left from the Chapel of the Teutonic Knights we soon reach arch-spanned Blutgasse. This corner has gruesome memories. In the days of Rudolph von Habsburg, two noblemen, Count von Leiningen and Sir Kranich, ambushed some Viennese burghers known for their pro-Ottokar sentiments on their way home from some near-by tavern. Before their could call for help the two "noble" ruffians had cut off their heads. They left their victims lying at the corner of Blutgasse, heads neatly set on their corpses and this was how the neighbours found them next morning. Supposedly Rudolph himself passed by and happened to hear Leiningen whisper to Kranich: "You've made a mistake. You put the wrong head on the wrong body," which gave them away as the murderers. But since they had ostensibly done it for Rudolph's sake, they got off lightly in the end.

Across the road is the Palais Neupauer-Breuner and a quick glance into its balconied court is worth-while.

Now let us turn into Blutgasse.

Blutgasse

A strange name—"Blood Lane"—and one of that is still something of a mystery. Between 1369 and 1411, this lane appears under the name of Khotgessl (Mud Lane), which leaves little doubt as to its condition. It was not until 1542, that the present name crops up. Legend has it that the blood to which it refers was that of the Templar Knights. When their Order was abolished in 1312, they are supposed to have been slaughtered in their headquarters, which where located just off Blutgasse in the Fähnrichshof (see p. 34). So many knights found their death that the street was a river of blood.

Recent research traces "Blut" to the Germanic "bluot"—a sacrificial offering and this, in turn, has led to the assumption that some pagan shrine was once located here.

This complex of buildings is probably one of the best examples of the great charm of well-renovated houses. For a while, it seemed that the buildings on Blutgasse would all have to be condemned; they were, in very bad state of repair and neither the owners, nor the Office for the Preservation of Monuments were in a position to invest the money necessary for their restoration. Then the City Council came up with a solution, announcing it would restore the original facade of the buildings, if the prospective owners would finance the renovation of their apartments at their own expense. Many famous people—opera singers, actors, physicians and lawyers—rose to the challenge and it was through their participation that the entire Fähnrichshof (16th century) was restored to its previous splendour. Inside, the apartments feature every modern convenience, while the courtyards give an excellent impression of what Vienna must have looked like in days gone by.

Let us enter No. 9. To the right, a narrow winding staircase, now closed off, is visible. To the left a vaulted space opens up which was, no doubt, once a shop or workshop. Coming into the light-well, we look up at four stories of balconies typical of what is called a Pawlatschenhaus. The word requires an explanation: this kind of

The plane tree in the Fähnrichshof

house was built around an inner court or light-well with the different apartments connected by long, narrow open corridors. The name originated from the Czech word 'pavlač', meaning an open gallery.

Steps leading down to three levels of cellars are also visible. A modern elevator is discreetly hidden away on the other side.

At the back to the left, there is a dark little passage which takes us out into the courtyard, the Fähnrichshof (Ensigns' Court), so called because it was here that the citizens of this district gathered around their flag in times of unrest or danger. The court was once part of the nearby nunnery of St. Niclas, of which nothing but the name of a dead-end street remains.

This quadrangle lies in the shadow of a plane tree, a lovely old specimen which, in its younger day, must have been enclosed by an iron fence. The tree eventually burst its limitations and now two rusty remnants of the fence protrude from its mighty trunk. Nevertheless, the tree stands tall and strong, in defiance of this minor injury, which could do little to deter its growth.

In the far right-hand corner of this court there are steps leading down and we follow them into yet another court. Here, turning sharply to the left, we ascend a few steps which, in turn, lead to a third and finally fourth court, belonging to No. 3 Blutgasse. This without doubt, is the finest Pawlatschenhaus in the city and extremely picturesque, especially in the summer when it is overgrown with creeper.

The complex houses various shops and art galleries and has the distinction of having been the first pedestrian zone in Vienna.

We walk out on to Blutgasse once more and turn right until we reach Domgasse.

Domgasse

The name needs little explanation being right behind the Cathedral (Dom).

House No. 5, opposite Blutgasse, is the famous Figaro House where Mozart lived from 1784–1787. With his family, he occupied the entire first floor. Unfortunately, the rent was exorbitant and, after only three years, he had to move on to cheaper lodgings on Landstrasse. As the name of the house suggests, it was here that Mozart wrote–among many other works–"The Marriage of Figaro". While he lived here, his teacher and friend Joseph Haydn visited him, as did Beethoven, who had come to Vienna expressly to see Mozart and to take lessons from him. Mozart is supposed to have said to friends once: "Keep an eye on him, he's going to make the world sit up some day."

Next door is the "King of Hungary Inn", now a hotel and restaurant. Its front door opens on to Schulerstrasse. The Domgasse side, until only a few years ago, used to have a marble slab saying "Das Vaterhaus" (The house of our fathers) and beneath it the following lines:

Three generations have now contributed
to the welfare of this dear old house:
grandfather, father and son–all in
the same trade. God bless our work!

Unfortunately, this plaque has meanwhile disappeared.

On the other side of the road at No. 6 we find the Small Bishop's Court, known at one time as the House of the Red Cross. What makes it memorable is that it belonged to the man who allegedly founded Vienna's first coffee house.

In 1683, during the second Turkish Siege of Vienna, a man by the name of Kolschitzky volunteered to go into the enemy camp to reconnoitre the situation, particularly whether there was any news of an approaching Polish relief army under King Sobiesky and Duke Karl von Lothringen, whom the Viennese were expecting to come to their aid. Kolschitzky was the ideal man for this mission, because before the war, as a merchant, he had travelled extensively in Turkey and knew the language. He did, in fact, manage to find out that the Polish army was on its way and by conveying this news to Vienna he was able to encourage the exhausted citizens to hold out just a few more days. When Sobiesky finally arrived, he put the Turkish army to flight and forced it to leave behind tents, ammunition and much else of their equipment.

Kolschitzky was celebrated as a hero and the Emperor asked him what he would like as a present. It didn't take the merchant long to answer that question. He asked for the many bags of strange green beans which had been found in the Turkish camp. As no one knew what they were, his wish was granted. In addition, he was given a house, the Small Bishop's Court. Kolschitzky knew only too well what to do with the beans. He roasted, ground and boiled them in water. This brew–later to be known as coffee–he originally served without milk and sugar in a small shop in the courtyard of his house.

The drink grew very popular and shortly the court at Domgasse became too small, so Kolschitzky moved to a new location, calling it "The Blue Bottle". He became very prosperous and soon other such coffee houses sprang up like mushrooms all over town and Vienna has been a city of coffee houses ever since. (See picture at the Museum of the First District p. 113)

This pretty story is only partly true. In fact it was an Armenian called Johann Diodate who was the first to sell the "oriental" brew in Vienna.

Grünangergasse

From Domgasse we turn into Grünangergasse (the street of the green fields or common). This area was once pasture land, where goats, geese and chickens were kept. The very first building on the right is the beautiful Palais Fürstenberg, with its graceful greyhounds over the portal. Some previous owner, with a most generous mind, had an ornate fireplace built in the hallway, presumably to keep his coachmen warm. As it now houses offices, it is only open during the week, but it is worth going in to see, not only the mantlepiece, but the elaborate ceiling above it and while there, take a brief look at the staircase.

Coming out of the Palais Fürstenberg it is advisable to cross the street for a better view of No. 8, which, for centuries, was the site of a bakery. Generation after generation of bakers lived and worked on these premises and to this day it is known as the "Brotbäckenhaus" (bread baker's house). A delightful relief over its entrance shows the many varieties of baked goods turned out in the past, and with one exception, they are still to be found in Viennese bakery shops today.

The story goes that this is the birthplace of the Kipfel, the croissant, which was supposed to have been invented to ridicule the Turks and their half-moon emblem after their defeat at the 1683 Siege of Vienna. However, there is a much earlier reference to the Kipfel, dating back to the 13th century, when such a pastry was presented to the reigning Duke at Christmas-tide.

The bakery goods depicted on the relief from left to right and top to bottom are: Bosniakerl, Schusterlaberl (shoe-maker's roll), Kipfel, Bretzel, Beugl (usually filled with either nuts or poppyseed) and Girafferl (a little giraffe).

The courtyard here is also very pretty and features a gen-uine "Bassena", a tap and basin, such as used to be found on every floor in apartment houses, and serving as the only replacement of the medieval well. Even though no longer the sole water supply, they can still be seen in many Viennese houses.

The Italian restaurant "All' Ancora Verde" is located at No. 10. Its founder must have thought that the name of the street referred to a "green anchor" instead of a green field. The restaurant itself is over two hundred years old, though, and can boast of having counted Schubert, Brahms and the painters Klimt and Schiele among its guests.

Franziskanerplatz

This is one of the most recent squares in the city, dating back only to 1624. Prior to that time, a house stood on this site. However, when the Franciscan Order–the ol-dest order of mendicant friars–established itself in the erstwhile convent of St. Jerome, the new church they built became very popular, especially among the aristocracy. By 1621, their Prior addressed himself to the Emperor with the request that the old house be pulled down as there was no place near the church where carriages could wait for their patrons–parking problems even in those days! Now the statue of Moses stands on top of the fountain in the centre of the square. All around it cars are parked, so I doubt if churchgoers are any better off than they were in the 17th century.

Though "young", the square gives an impression of age, for the majority of the houses were built before 1650, which gives a certain unity to the entire complex.

Let us enter the church. On the High Altar there is a statue of the Virgin: St. Mary with the Axe. It is carved out of lime-wood and the axe protrudes from the statue's left shoulder. Legend has it, that originally is stood in a monastery in Bohemia. This monastery was later turned into a residence for Count Sternberg, but the statue remained in the chapel. The count's heirs turned Protestant and one of them ordered the statue to be burnt. To everybody's amazement it jumped out of the flames unscathed and was found the next day in its old place in the chapel. The Count than ordered the village executioner to chop it up, but this, too, proved impossible–the axe stuck in the shoulder and could not be removed. It must have been given up as a bad job, for the next thing we hear of the statue is that the Count's son, turned Catholic again in the counter-Reformation, returned it to its former place of honour and later gave it to the Franciscan Friars, in whose possession the miracle-working Virgin has been since 1607.

In two of the chapels, one on the right and one on the left aisle, there are coffins made of glass, containing the relics of two martyrs, St. Hilaria and St. Felix. These were brought to Vienna about 1720. Hilaria is a wax figure, holding the relics of the saint, whereas Felix is merely a skeleton clothed like a Roman centurion.

On the right, there is also a rather unusual depiction of the death of St. John Nepomuk. He is floating on the waters of the River Moldava (for the respective legend see p. 97).

We leave the church and make our way to the monastery next door. In the 14th century, it was a convent for penitents, to which women, who had led sinful lives, could retire to repent. At first these women lived here in seclusion, not bound by any vows. They could follow any respectable occupation and were even able to marry under the special protection of the reigning monarch, thus becoming very popular as spouses.

Later all the women took the vow of obedience, while some, such as the Abbess and those in charge of the dormitories, also vowed lifetime poverty and chastity. They called themselves the Order of St. Mary Magdalene. For over two centuries this convent flourished, supported by gifts from the citizens of Vienna. But the Reformation and a fire in 1525 were the beginning of its downfall. By 1543, there were only eight women and the Abbess left and their way of life had strayed far from the straight and narrow path of virtue. The Mother Superior, one Juliane Kleeberger, even went as far as to have an affair with the convent's priest Laubinger. Complaints about this state of affairs arose, so Laubinger married the Abbess in a self-conducted ceremony.

Their conjugal life, however, was not happy for long as Laubinger was soon plagued by jealousy, accusing the few remaining nuns of aiding and abetting his "wife" and, in a fit of pique, excommunicated the lot of them.

After having squandered most of the convent's funds, the pair were finally arrested. Yet the citizens of Vienna felt sorry for them and insisted on their release. Thereupon Laubinger disappeared, while Juliane returned to the convent where she died in 1553. Her tombstone can still be seen in the "Tummelplatz" (recreation room) in front of the sacristy. The inscription bears no mention of her rather "unholy life", but calls her the "Honourable" Mother Superior.

The Order, however, never quite recovered and by 1589 the convent was handed over to the Franciscan Friars who then proceeded to reconstruct much of it as well as

The Organ in the Monks' Choir of the Franciscan Monastery

the adjoining church where the first mass was said in 1607.

Here I cannot resist telling you of my own adventures in this monastery. I had read that there is supposed to be a

41

beautiful, richly carved Baroque organ (built 1642 by Johann Wöckerl); however, I had seen no trace of it in the church. So one day I ventured into the monastery and my first reaction on reaching the cloisters was one of shock: for on the right, just inside the door, there was a skull leering at me. On closer investigation it turned out to be a marble holy water font, made in the shape of a skull. Unfortunately, this rather sombre memento mori has meanwhile been replaced by a very ordinary font, which inspires neither fear nor even piety. But you can still decypher the words underneath "Heute an mir – morgen an dir" (My turn today–your turn tomorrow) which, of course, refers to the deathhead and its reminder of our mortality.

The first impression inside the cloisters is one of peace. On the wall there are repeated requests for silence. The noise of the street is barely audible and all one can hear is the bird-song in the quadrangle. I went to the porch, which is at the left, rang the bell and soon a young boy of about twelve looked out of the small window. Yes, he said, I might see the organ. Would I go halfway round the cloisters, where he would meet me. This I did and he appeared almost immediately through another door. He unlocked what turned out to be the entrance to the erstwhile "Tummelplatz". The first thing that strikes the eye is a fantastic confessional (first half of the 18th century), some very ancient tombstones, and the tombstone of Juliane Kleebergerin, as she is called here.

The boy bade me follow. We went through another doorway and found ourselves behind the altar. And there, in the so-called monks' choir, was one of the most lovely organs I have ever seen. It is richly carved with a comparatively small keyboard. The pipes are flanked by painted wings like those of an altar and crowned by King David playing the harp accompanied by two angelic musicians. Truly this is a queen of instruments!

Just as the boy was switching on the light so that I could get a better look at it, a young, fair-haired novice, with a large blue apron appeared. "Wouldn't you like to hear it?" he asked. What a question! Of course, I wanted to hear it and so he sat down, telling the boy to work the bellows at the back. I felt a little guilty seeing the poor boy working away so hard, but soon forgot him when the organ burst into song.

Lured by the music, another young, dark-haired novice entered and immediately the organist turned and said: "Oh, come here, you play it, you're so much better at it than I am." The newcomer did not need much persuading; perhaps it was the monastery's organist himself. The other novice went to take over from the boy who seemed relieved. The musician sat down and, pulling the stops expertly, began a magnificent performance, making the entire church resound. I was spellbound: a mini-concert just for me. I was overwhelmed by the idea that such a glorious instrument still gives forth a sweet sound after so many years and not merely a hoarse wheeze. They told me afterwards that the organ is in a bad state of repair and that so far they have been unable to raise the necessary funds for it. But it is still used.

"And someone has to work the bellows all the time?" I asked. "Oh no, it works by electricity now, only we haven't got the key to the box," confided the novice.

In the old days the monks–or rather the brothers as they like to be called–used to hold their offices in this choir. There is an old lectern with a strange arm sticking out above it which, at one time, held a lantern to enable the reader to see.

You, too, can ask for permission to see the organ and if the time does not conflict with the monastic offices or their meals I am sure this permission will be granted.

Let us leave this other-world atmosphere and go out into the square again. We cross Weihburggasse to the archway which leads into Ballgasse. Before passing under it, though, take a brief look at the house to the left. It has two beautiful wrought-iron balconies (18th century).

Ballgasse

The name is derived from a ball house that once stood here. The ball game, a kind of badminton, had been introduced to Austria by Ferdinand I, who brought it from Spain.

We enter the lane from Franziskanerplatz by way of a long, dark, tunnel-like archway which leads into a narrow, winding street. Here one can well imagine what city streets must have been like in the past.

No. 8 is the site of the ball house. After the ball game went out of fashion, the house was rented out to Italian strolling players and, in 1772, it became the inn where the Carpenter Guild housed its journeymen. This is commemorated by a sign over the door.

The journeymen, though no longer required to live with their respective master's family, were expected to stay at inns recommended by the Guild. This they greatly resented and it had been one of the causes of the Shoemakers' Rebellion in 1721.

Across the way, another side street branches off. This is Blumenstockgasse which can be traced back to a very popular beer house "The Old Flower Pot". It was in this tavern that some writers and artists founded a club in 1818 they called "Ludlamshöhle". The club soon became so popular that they had to move to other premises. The Old Flower Pot, in turn, grew too small to accomodate its clients and moved to a larger building across the way, calling itself "The New Flower Pot". Even today it is still in the same line of business, though it is now a well-known restaurant.

We stay on Ballgasse which runs into Rauhensteingasse.

Rauhensteingasse

This appelation is probably connected with the Criminal Court which had its quarters at No. 10: "Rauhenhaus" (the rough place). I do not doubt that things were pretty rough, for the inmates of its dungeons were both tortured and hanged there. In 1603, a woman threw herself down the well in the courtyard because she had been accused of sorcery and was so terrified of being tortured that she preferred a quick death. Witches could not be burnt according to a then prevalent superstition, so they put them in barrels and threw them into the Danube to be carried away downstream.

At one time the house where Mozart died in 1791 stood on this street No. 8. Now it has been incorporated into a large department store. The following story is told in connection with his death:

When Mozart was already suffering from the illness that was to lead to his untimely death, a gentleman in grey came to see him. The visitor commissioned Mozart to compose a Requiem Mass, however, he made it a condition that it be kept absolutely secret and Mozart had to promise never to inquire who his mysterious customer was. A down payment was made and the caller left. Mozart, very busy on his "Magic Flute", postponed work on the Requiem until one day the grey gentleman reappeared, urging him to deliver the promised work. So Mozart started on what was to be his last composition. On the afternoon of the day he died, Mozart suddenly realized that he would be unable to finish the Requiem and burst into tears. Later he gave his disciple, Süssmayr, detailed instructions as to the completion of the missing parts of the Mass, saying: "Didn't I tell you, this is to be my own Requiem?"

The grey gentleman proved to be Graf Franz von Walsegg. He commissioned the Requiem for his deceased wife. It seems he had long been accustomed to have renowned musicians compose for him. He then had their works performed at his residence in Styria, pretending they were his own.

Himmelpfortgasse

On Rauhensteingasse we turn left and shortly arrive at Himmelpfortgasse which owes its name to the convent that stood at Nos. 7–11.

The Convent of the Gates of Heaven owned a very famous statue of the Virgin Mary for many years (see p. 14 Hausmutter in St. Stephen's, St. Eligius Chapel). When the dissolution of the convent was ordered by Joseph II in 1783 the statue was transferred to St. Stephen's. There is a legend connected with this statue:

According to the convent rules, a nun was chosen to act as portress (doorkeeper). She was the only one of all the inmates of the convent who had some contact with the outside world. At one time the nun chosen for this task happened to be young and pretty. Temptation came to her in the form of a handsome young knight, who tried to persuade her to break her vows and follow him. At first the young nun resisted but finally she succumbed and, laying the keys of the great gate at the feet of the statue of the Virgin, she prayed fervently: "Guard your house, Mother Mary, I am no longer able to do so" and left the convent.

At first the young woman was happy, living a life of luxury and ease. But after a few years, her lover abandoned her and she soon became poor and sick. After a long inner struggle, she decided to return to the convent. A humble and repentant sinner, she pulled the bell at the gate. Great was her surprise when it was opened by a nun who looked exactly as she once had. It was no other than the Virgin Mary herself, who had taken her place at the gate since that night and had done the duties of a portress so that the other nuns had never noticed the young nun's absence.

On Himmelpfortgasse itself, we turn left again and a few steps further down, on the other side of the street at No. 8, we find ourselves face to face with Prince Eugene's Winter Palace, now the Ministry of Finance. This is probably the most elaborate of all the town places once belonging to the Austrian aristocracy. Two of the most famous Baroque architects are responsible for its construction: Fischer von Erlach and Lukas von Hildebrandt. The magnificent staircase is the work of the former. Whereas the rest of the palace can only be viewed on the occasion of a tour, and these tours are few and far between, the staircase is open to the public. Let us therefore enter the vestibule through the mighty doorway. To the left, a Neptune is emptying a shell–no doubt used as a fountain at one time–and straight ahead there is a courtyard with another small fountain against the wall.

But it is to the right that we must turn to mount the staircase. It is carried by atlantes and halfway up a huge Hercules stands, swinging his club. At the back there is a relief portrait of Prince Eugene, flanked by the labours of Hercules.

In all this splendour, Prince Eugene is supposed to have occupied a suite facing the courtyard "very peaceful and quiet", because from what we know of his love of simplicity and horror of pomp, it would seem likely that he only used the sumptuous hall facing Himmelpfortgasse for official purposes.

No. 13, further down the street, is another town palace belonging to the Erdödy-Fürstenberg family. As a commemorative tablet on the wall indicates, the Hungarian Duke Rákóczi used to stay here when he visited Vienna. Francis, Prince Rákóczi, fought as a rebel against the Habsburg Empire from 1703–1707. He was proclaimed Prince of Hungary, where he was extremely popular. Later, however, he was exiled, living in Poland, France and finally in Turkey, where he died in 1735.

No. 15 is a very pretty house with a gable and Renaissance entrance. During the week you can walk into its two charming courtyards, which the antique shop at the back has enhanced with some of its treasures.

Walking down to the end of the street, we come to Seilerstätte.

Seilerstätte (1)

After the second Turkish Siege the rope-makers had their quarters here until about the middle of the 18th century, when it became a most frequented egg and poultry market. The smell at that time must have been overwhelming. A contemporary complained: "Long after leaving this ear-piercing and nose-offending district ... one still believes oneself in this crowd of men, women and birds, the eardrums still vibrate with the thousand-fold cackling of the chickens and the smelling organs are still offended by their mephitic emanations."

Coming out of Himmelpfortgasse we see a monumental building on the other side of Seilerstätte. At the turn of the century, it was a famous music hall which incorporated, besides the theatre itself, a hotel, a restaurant, a coffee house and a ballroom. It was called "Ronacher" after its founder and director, and gained such a reputation in its field, attracting not only world-famous artists, but also the cream of society as an audience, that the name still holds precious memories for the older generation to this day.

From 1945–1955 it housed the bombed-out Burgtheater-Ensemble. At the time of writing the Ronacher is being restored to serve as a theatre once more.

We now turn right until we come to Johannesgasse.

Johannesgasse

We will take just a few steps down this street for on the right at No. 15, there is one of those unexpected jewels of a courtyard. A beautiful statue of the Immaculate Virgin over the door greets us as we enter. In summer, the trees in this court give the weary pedestrian some welcome shade and a bench provides repose for a few minutes. At the further end a fountain depicts the biblical

The Widow of Sarepta

story of Elisha and the widow of Sarepta: "Elisha maketh a widow rich in oil" says the writing above it.
This peaceful environment was indeed for many years a place of retirement for aristocratic widows, known as the Savoyan Gentlewomen's Foundation. At one time the

house belonged to Prince Eugene's nephew and his widow left instructions in her will that it be turned into a home for widowed ladies.

Both the fountain and the statue of the Virgin on the front of the house are the work of Franz Xaver Messerschmidt (1736–1783), a sculptor famous for a series of grimacing old men, now exhibited at the Barockmuseum in the Lower Belvedere.

Back to the street. On the other side is the chapel of what was once the Convent of the Ursuline Nuns. Until quite recently this was a well-known girls' school. It now houses part of the Academy of Music and Performing Arts. The little chapel dates back to 1675 and on Sunday masses are still celebrated.

Back to Seilerstätte, we continue along until we reach corner of Krugerstrasse.

Seilerstätte (2)

Although our tour will later take us back to Annagasse, we now pause at this corner to take in the phenomenal view: there, spread out before you, is Schwarzenbergplatz with Prince Schwarzenberg astride his horse. In the distance you can see a tall column, although from here it is hard to make out what it is. The statue on top of it represents a Russian soldier and is a memento the Soviets left the Viennese after World War II. However, this parting gift is not much appreciated and often referred to as the "Memorial to the Unknown Plunderer".

During the summer months there is a lovely fountain just in front of the monument, the Hochstrahlbrunnen (the high spouting fountain), which is illuminated at night. An amusing poem in a Viennese periodical once asked facetiously what the Water Works thought they were doing. Couldn't they turn the fountain up a little higher to hide the monument? Or if that wasn't possible, could they not turn it a little sideways, so the water would in time erode that soldier down to the size of a Michelin manikin?

Rather marred by this monument and the colonnade behind it, now barely visible, is the Palais Schwarzenberg– one of the most sumptuous of the Viennese palaces and still the home of this ancient aristocratic family. One wing has been turned into a hotel. In the main building there are two lovely halls where concerts are occasionally performed.

And on a clear day you can even make out the green rooftops of the Belvedere Palace, Prince Eugene's summer residence.

Now let us retrace our steps along Seilerstätte as far as Annagasse.

Annagasse

The church, which gave it its name, is at the other end of the street; at one time there was a convent next to it. There is no doubt that this is one of the most charming streets in town. Practically every house is eighteenth century, some even older.

We have no sooner turned into Annagasse than we find on our left a palace, the Erzherzog Karl. It is not one of the more spectacular palaces, but it is the building that saw Vienna's first Christmas tree. The very popular Princess Henriette von Nassau-Weilburg, wife of the same Archduke Charles for whom the palace was named, brought this tradition to Vienna in 1816. The tree, with its candles and decorations, so delighted the Viennese artists and aristocracy that the next year many of them followed her example. Today there is hardly a Viennese family which does not have its traditional Christmas tree. On the other side of the street, at No. 7, is the Mailbergerhof. It belonged to Bishop Kollonitz and later, in

The Sign of the Blue Carp

1775, came into the possession of the Knights of Malta. The wooden door still features the Maltese cross.

We wend our way up the street, criss-crossing from side to side. No. 14 was once a restaurant called the Blue Carp and you can still see the fish and name on the facade, moreover it has a delightful frieze of dancing cherubs.

Back again to the right side where we find the Kleinmariazellerhof and next to it, the Church of St. Anne.

Since 1320, this had been the site of a chapel, though the present church is 17th century. On the first side altar to the left–usually in semi-darkness–there is a wood-carved statue of St. Anne with the Virgin Mary and the Christ Child. It dates back to about 1510 and is possibly the work of Veit Stoss. This church also possesses a very special relique, a bone from the hand of St. Anne, which is exposed on the altar on St. Anne's day, July 26.

We pass the 17th century Kremsmünster-Hof (No. 4) and reach Kärntner Strasse.

Kärntner Strasse

Well, here we are on Vienna's main street. It is actually a very old one, mentioned as early as 1257, by which time it was obviously already well established as the main route to the seaports of Venice and Trieste. Today there is little left to remind us of its age. The 19th century is largely to blame and what little did remain was destroyed in the chaos of the last days of April 1945.

One of the few survivors is the Esterházy Palais at the corner of Annagasse and Kärntner Strasse (No. 41), which can at least claim to be early 18th century. It also houses one of Vienna's most famous couturiers.

Since the street has recently been turned into a pedestrian zone, it has become a favourite promenade for Viennese and tourists alike. In the summer the side-walk cafés are very popular and the possibility of window-shopping without being disturbed by the pollution and noise of heavy traffic is extremely tempting.

Our tour takes us to the right and almost immediately we come to the Malteser Kirche, the church of the Knights of Malta. The outside belies its age because the facade is early 19th century, but if you step inside you will find 15th century vaults, a pretty 18th century organ and many coats-of-arms of members of this knighthood, among them illustrious names of the Austrian nobility.

After leaving the church, we go to the end of the block, cross Kärntner Strasse and walk up a short lane, Marco d'Aviano-Gasse which leads us to Neuer Markt.

Neuer Markt

Having arrived on Neuer Markt, we are practically facing the Capuchin Monastery and its adjoining church. It is in the crypt of this church that the bodies of the Habsburg dynasty have been buried since the time of Emperor

Maria Theresa's tomb

Matthias and his wife Anna. The only exception to this august company is Maria Theresa's governess, Countess Fuchs. When objections were raised, Maria Theresa is supposed to have answered: "She was always with us in life, she shall be with us in death, too."

In all, there are 142 coffins in the crypt. The double coffin of Maria Theresa and her husband Franz, depicts the couple in a very life-like posture–as if they were both just waking up in the morning (though it is their awakening at the last Judgement that the sculptor had in mind). Maria Theresa loved her husband very much in spite of his repeated infidelities. After he died, she used to visit his tomb frequently and in later years, due to her corpulence, an elevator had to be installed down to the crypt to spare her the effort of descending and mounting the stairs. On November 20, 1780, when she was once again on a visit to the burial vault, the elevator stalled three times on the way up and when she finally reached the top Maria Theresa said: "It seems to me that the crypt doesn't want to let me go." It was to be her last visit; she died on November 29.

At the foot of that enormous rococo double tombstone lies her son, Joseph II, in an austere, unpretentious coffin–a blatant contrast in death as in life. A few days before he died, he told his secretary that he wanted the following epitaph to be inscribed on his tomb: "Here lies Joseph II, who failed in everything he untertook". Needless to say, his successor ignored this wish, not wanting to perpetuate the resignation with which the dying Emperor looked back on his life.

It is said that when a monarch died and his body was taken to the crypt, the herald would step forward and knock on the door. The monk inside would ask who desired to enter. The first time the answer was "The Emperor"–but the door remained closed. Again the herald would knock and this time the answer to the same question was "The King"–and again there was no admittance. Finally, the herald knocked a third time and upon being asked who was there, answered humbly: "A poor sinner", whereupon the great door was thrown open and the coffin could be taken to its last resting place.

Back to Neuer Markt itself. It was once the corn and flour market. In very early days (15th century), it was often the scene of tournaments and races, and later plays were performed here. In Maria Theresa's reign, a delightful winter pastime became popular among the aristocracy: sleigh rides. Should you go to visit Schloss Schönbrunn, be sure not to miss the Wagenburg (the carriage house), where the royal carriages are on display.

Among these are some pretty sleighs, their horses covered with little bells–yes, one can imagine them sweeping round the square in the winter twilight, the ladies all bundled up in furs. The last of these sleigh rides took place in the Winter of 1814/15 during the Vienna Congress, in which most of the monarchs in Europe participated.

In the centre of the square is the famous fountain by Georg Raphael Donner. Providence sits at the top surrounded by four Austrian rivers: Enns, March, Traun and Ybbs. During Maria Theresa's reign, the much feared chastity commission–a police force appointed specifically to supervise public morality–declared the figures lewd because they were naked and had them removed in 1770. For 31 years they lay hidden away in some depot. Then they were offered to the sculptor Johann Martin Fischer as lead to be melted down for his use. He luckily recognised their worth and was able to have them reinstated in 1801. The present fountain is a bronze copy of the original, which is now on display at the Baroque Museum at the Belvedere.

We walk the entire length of the square and finally end up on the left side in Seilergasse.

Kärntner Durchgang

We will not linger on Seilergasse, as there is little more to be said about it than that it was the street where the rope-makers had their shops.

The first little lane branching off to the right is called Kärntner Durchgang (a passage that leads to Kärntner Strasse). The present road was only created when a house was torn down here in 1898. Short as it is, it houses a bar (Kärntner Bar), which was designed by the famous architect Adolf Loos in 1908 and is often, even today, referred to as "Loosbar". Unfortunately, little is

One of the statues from the Donner Fountain

left of the original design. In the early fifties of this century, the cellar of this establishment became very famous as the "Art Club". Young artists, musicians and writers of the time frequented it and any visiting celebrity would invariably end up his evening there. Apart from being a tavern, it was also used for exhibitions, recitals and poetry readings. The well-known pianist Friedrich Gulda would often drop in after a concert and spend the rest of the night playing jazz. In 1952, after their performance of "Porgy and Bess", the entire cast including William Warfield, Cab Calloway and Leontyne Price, gave an impromtu concert there till the early hours of the morning. It is a great pity that this club no longer exists.

A few steps further and we come out into Kärntner Strasse. From here, turning left, it is only a block to St. Stephen's Square.

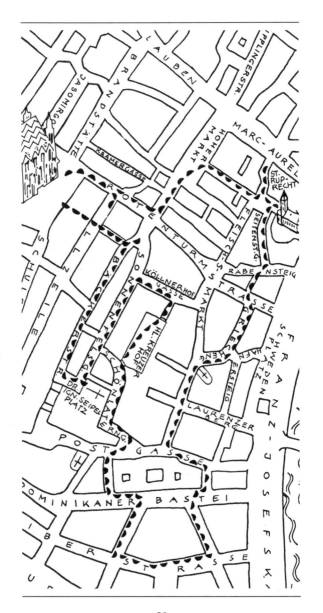

THIRD TOUR

Rotenturmstrasse
Lichtensteg/Kramergasse
Hoher Markt
Judengasse
Sterngasse
Ruprechtsplatz
Seitenstettengasse
Griechengasse
Fleischmarkt
Otto Wagner's Postsparkasse
Schönlaterngasse
Heiligenkreuzerhof
Sonnenfelsgasse
Dr.-Ignaz-Seipel-Platz
Bäckerstrasse
Lugeck

Rotenturmstrasse

Facing the main gate of St. Stephen's Cathedral, we head left down Rotenturmstrasse. This "Street of the Red Tower" once led to a red tower–or to be exact, a red-white checked tower–one of the fortified town gates by an arm of the Danube, which at that time flowed roughly where the Danube Canal now cuts through the city.

There is an amusing story connected with this tower. Someone had hung a nice, juicy piece of bacon high on the side of the building, with a parchment attached to it, offering it as a prize to "the least henpecked man in town". Many a man slunk away not even trying his luck, until a brawny shoemaker appeared on the scene and claimed the side of bacon for himself. He was no henpecked husband–not he! And to prove it he stripped off his coat and prepared to climb the tower. But at the last minute he hesitated: "Maybe I'd better not," he mused, "my wife will be furious if I get my trousers dirty!"

Immediately on the right of Rotenturmstrasse is the Archbishop's Palace, but in order to see its fine courts one must turn at the corner of Wollzeile and enter by way of No. 2. As the courts are now closed off, you must go to the doorman and ask him to open the gate for you. The first court has a spectacular view of both the unfinished and the great South Tower of St. Stephen's rising above the roof of the palace. The second court to the right brings you, rather surprisingly, face to face with a very pretty young maiden, sitting with what looks very much like a wine pitcher and gaily raising a goblet in her right hand. When I first encountered this damsel, I wondered how she had found her way into this episcopal environment. Later I realized that I had grossly misjudged her. She is an allegorical figure representing Temperance–true her pitcher yields nothing but water–and usually not even that. The first of the two courtyards is the site of one of Vienna's oldest legends. Here stood the first parsonage of the parish of St. Stephen's, a much humbler building than today's palace. When the old

The lady in the Archbishop's Palace

Romanesque parish church was to be enlarged into a Gothic church, some of the trees surrounding it were to be moved and an old linden tree would have had to be cut down. The parish priest was deeply concerned about the threatened removal of the lovely tree outside his window. All these many years, winter and summer, the tree had been his companion and he hated the thought of missing its familiar silhouette or the rustle of its leaves. However, the master mason was a kind man and the priest managed to persuade him to spare his tree. And so they grew old together, the priest and his beloved linden. When the priest was far gone in years, he fell ill one winter and his housekeeper feared that he would not live to see the spring. One bitter January night the old man's mind began to wander–or so the housekeeper thought–for he was babbling about his lovely linden tree. Suddenly he sat up in bed and begged her to open the window so he could smell the fragrant blossoms once more. The horrified woman refused, fearing the icy air would surely hasten his death. But the priest would not be pacified and with his last strength rose from his bed and staggered to the window, throwing it wide open. And out there, amidst all the snow, the linden stood in full bloom. The old man took one long breath, inhaling its intoxicating fragrance, then slid noiselessly to the floor. When the housekeeper reached his side it was too late, he was dead, but on his face there was a beatific smile.

Lichtensteg/Kramergasse

Back to Rotenturmstrasse we next reach Lichtensteg, a short lane leading off to the left. Pause a while in front of the pharmacy "Zum Roten Krebs" (The Red Crayfish). It takes us back to the times when crayfish was one of the main delicacies on the nearby fish market. By the middle of the 16th century this was the most fashionable pharmacy in town and the Court Supplier. It was also the first pharmacy to sell homeopathic medicines–and still does to this day.

On the left, corner of Kramergasse, there was once what was known as the "Bretzeneck" (Pretzel Corner), because even as far back as 1391 pretzels were being sold there. Before turning our attention to Hoher Markt and its sights, let us briefly enter Kramergasse. At the end of the first block on the right is a shop specializing in basket ware. It has some most remarkable showrooms: no less than four cellars, one under the other. If you descend down, down, down into the lower depths of Vienna, you can see some ancient vaulting and next to the stairs leading to the last cellar, even remnants of a very old well. This certainly confirms what Aeneas Silvius Piccolomini, later Pope Pius II, wrote about Vienna around 1450: "The wine cellars are so deep and extensive that one could say there is a second city of Vienna underground."

Hoher Markt

This is beyond a doubt the oldest square in Vienna. It was the site of the original Roman Camp Vindobona and the remains of this camp can be seen in the cellar of house No. 3. This small exhibition is well worth a visit as it shows, among other things, the amazing central-heating system used in the 2nd century A. D., as well as examples of bricks stamped with the seals of the various legions who served here.

The square crops up again during the 13th century, when chronicles already referred to it as "the Old Market". It was indeed a centre, for all the most important guildhalls were located around it, those of the shoemakers, the linen weavers, the candlemakers and the skinners.

Coming from Kramergasse, you turn left on Hoher Markt and at the next corner, look across the square to an archway spanning Rotgasse, where you will see a clock: Ankeruhr. It was constructed between 1911–1917 by Franz Matsch for the Anker Insurance Company. In order to get the full benefit of this clockwork in action you should try to be there just before 12 noon, when the entire assembly of figures march by to music, each with a signature tune of its own.

The figures of the Anker clock represent:

1. Marcus Aurelius
2. Charlemagne
3. Leopold the Glorious and his Consort Theodora

The "Anker" Clock

4. Walther von der Vogelweide
5. Duke Rudolph the Founder
6. Master builder Hans Puchsbaum
7. Maximilian I (the Last Knight)
8. Mayor Liebenberg (1680–1683)
9. Rüdiger von Starhemberg
10. Prince Eugene
11. Maria Theresa and Francis I
12. Joseph Haydn

Today the large yet graceful "Vermählungsbrunnen" (Wedding Fountain), designed by Fischer von Erlach sen. and built by his son, dominates the square. It replaced the pillory and gallows originally situated there. Leopold I had sworn to dedicate a monument to St. Joseph if his eldest son (later Joseph I) turned safely and victoriously from the Siege of Landau. It depicts the marriage of Joseph and Mary.

The entire block between Judengasse and Marc Aurel Strasse at the far end of the square was at one time occupied by a single building, the Berghof. By the end of the 13th century it was already known as the oldest house in Vienna and was considered to have been the first building from which the city later grew. It was demolished in the 17th century.

But probably the most important building there was for many centuries the "Schranne"–the Court House. It was built in 1440 and stood at the corner of Tuchlauben and Hoher Markt. Somewhat later it went down in history for its broad staircase leading to the first floor, on the landing of which the judge would emerge to proclaim the death sentences. The court building also had its own chapel, "Christ's Death Agony Chapel" as it was appropriately called, and the "Armesünderglöcklein" (Poor Sinner's Bell) would toll when a culprit was led away to execution.

Across the way was the "Narrenkotterl", cages in which madmen, prostitutes, witches, fortune-tellers and drunkards were displayed to the jeering crowds. In 1710 it was torn down and replaced by a "modern" pillory.

The main function of the square, however, was that of a market, specializing in fish and crayfish. A fishery law dated February 1516 quaintly states: "Para. 6–No one may sell fish who is not a citizen and does not have a wedded wife." One wonders why bachelors were not allowed to sell fish. In its centre there was a fountain called the Fish Fountain which, by the middle of the 16th century, had its own water supply flowing from four pipes. This water came all the way from Hernals (now one of the outer districts of Vienna) in order to supply enough fresh water for the live fish sold at the market.

The square lent itself ideally to festivities such as the "Johannesfeuer" (a mixture of the pagan midsummernight celebration and the Christian feast of St. John the Baptist). It is first recorded in 1481, but was probably quite old by then. A fine sight it must have been, too: first the City Counsellors arriving on their horses, followed by drummers and pipers. Then came the sparsely clad "Hübschlerinnen" (Pretties), also referred to as the "free daughters", both being euphemisms for the town prostitutes, and finally the craftsmen. Very soon all would be dancing around a big fire. Wine flowed very freely and the merry-making usually turned into a regular Bacchanalia. In 1524 it was forbidden by the police.

To the right of the Fountain we turn into Judengasse.

Judengasse

Originally all streets in the Jewish ghetto were simply called "Jew Lane"–as if they had no right to a name of their own. Along this street the Jewish second-hand clothes dealers had their quarters. Today there is not much to remind use of those times. True, most of the lively little shops still have the old shutters, but the stores that still use them, as for instance the one at No. 7, are few. These shutters with their iron cross-bars tell a grim tale of the periodical raids that took place here. How often did the words "They're coming . . ." cause a feverish activity among the merchants, who quickly shut and barred all doors and windows, withdrawing into some back room or cellar until the mob calmed down again. Sometimes, however, the situation was more serious and the Jews had to pack up and take to the road. They were driven out of the city in 1421, 1567, 1572, 1614 and again in 1670, not to mention their latest exodus in the years 1938/39. And it was only the lucky ones who escaped. Each one of these pogroms took a heavy toll of the Jewish population.

St. Barbara, Lazenhof

House No. 4, further up on Judengasse to your right, is an unprepossessing building—a typical 20th century tenement. But a statue of St. Barbara has been salvaged from a previous age and graces the wall. This complex has a name of its own, the last remnant of a large building that spread all the way to Bauernmarkt and at one time also included a beautiful garden: Lazenhof. In the 15th century the house was in the possession of the Laz family. The famous Viennese scholar, Wolfgang Laz (often referred to as Lazius), was born here in 1514. He became first Dean, then Chancellor of the University, but was also a very prominent man at Court. Ferdinand I made him both a counsellor and his personal physician, apart from which he was the Court historian and director of the Royal Mint. He was finally knighted for his services. The man was indeed the epitome of a Renaissance scholar. He was a great collector and the first in Vienna to preserve Roman tombstones and altars. These he put up in his garden or set them in the walls surrounding it. After he died in 1565, however, this marvellous collection was lost. His own tombstone is in Peterskirche (see p. 101).

House No. 7, at the corner of Sterngasse, was once the home of Vienna's famous "Plague Doctor", Dr. Sorbait. He left copious notes and prescriptions concerning the epidemic (see p. 79).

To the right there is an open space above the stairs that lead down to Fleischmarkt. From here you can see a strange, austere-looking tower with only a few small windows at the top. This building, having been erected between 1825–1827, can easily claim to be Vienna's first skyscraper. In its own time, it certainly looked down on the surrounding city.

The architect, Joseph Kornhäusel, conceived this forbidding edifice in order to escape his jealous wife's everlasting nagging. When he wanted a bit of peace and quiet he merely withdrew to his tower and if she insisted on following him, he would go to the top storey, pull up the drawbridge–its only means of access–and shut out all the unpleasantness and turmoil of everyday life. I will tell you more about this tower when we get to Seitenstettengasse (see p. 71). Right now let us turn down the dark, narrow lane to the left, Sterngasse.

Sterngasse

The name can be traced to a house sign: "The Dark Star". It seems that even stars were not bright in this dingy place.

The second house on the left, No. 3, is called the Wiener Neustädter Hof. There is a strange stone hanging beside the door and, as the writing informs us, this is a Turkish missile weighing 79 lbs, catapulted into the city on July 20, 1683. Miraculously, nobody was hurt and not much damage done.

From here a stairway leads down, but it is not worth descending as one gets quite a good view of the large boulder to the right of the stairs at the bottom from the street above. This is a reminder of Roman times, for it was used in one of their buildings and, after having been buried for many a century, it finally came to light again when the two houses, Nos. 5 and 7 Sterngasse, badly damaged in 1945, had to be torn down to make way for the large building at the corner. It is a great shame that these two houses could not be rescued, because both were 16th century. In fact, a considerable war raged between Viennese lovers of historic houses and the landlord concerned regarding their preservation. The street has one other attraction: it is the home of "Shakespeare & Co.", where book fiends will love to browse.

Let us retrace our steps to Judengasse, where we turn left.

Ruprechtsplatz

This name needs no explanation with St. Ruprecht's standing in the centre of the square. But even though, according to tradition the church has been there since 740, and is thus the oldest place of worship in town, the square around it is mentioned in 1246 under the name Torch Market where pine torches and resinous twigs, which were used as a means of illumination by the poor, were sold.

During an eclipse of the moon, on April 16, 1275, a terrible fire broke out in the square and practically all the surrounding houses were burnt, leaving only the church standing.

Now to the church: it is dedicated to a saint much fa-

St. Ruprecht's

voured by the See of Salzburg and it is therefore likely that it was the boatmen bringing salt up the Danube, who were responsible for its construction and considered it *their* church. The lower part of the tower consists of stones from the Roman fortification walls. The main aisle and the greater part of the tower are 11th century; some parts, certainly the foundations, are older–thus making it the only Romanesque church in Vienna.

Ruprechtsplatz No. 1 used to be the location of the so-called Prague House–where the name came from nobody knows. It has sometimes been assumed that it had something to do with the fact that King Wenceslas IV of Bohemia was held prisoner there. He and his brother Sigismund, King of Hungary, quarrelled; Sigismund captured Wenceslas and asked the Austrian Duke Albrecht IV to take him into custody. He was kept locked up at the Prague House for fifteen months. Finally, in 1403, he was able to escape with the help of a fisherman, who took him across the Danube in a boat.

There is another story connected with that house: Duke William had bought it in 1397. This peer had a strange pet: a tame lion who followed him everywhere. Once out riding, William fell from his horse and was brought to the Prague House where he soon succumbed to his injuries. The lion had taken his place by the bed and nothing could induce him to leave the body. Refusing all nourishment, the faithful animal finally died of grief by his master's side. We now retrace our steps Seitenstettengasse.

Seitenstettengasse

The Benedictine Abbey of Seitenstetten owns property there. The large building facing Franz-Josefs-Kai goes under the name of Seitenstettnerhof. Hence the name of this street, though I feel it would be more appropriate to call it Kornhäusel Street, as the majority of its houses were built by the architect Joseph Kornhäusel in the 1820's.

Two of them are of particular interest: the Synagogue and the Kornhäuselturm. Neither of them are visible from the street and both have been guarded by the police since the terrorist attack on August 29, 1982.

I have already mentioned the tower (see p. 68). However, I would like to recount my adventures while trying to find a means of entering it. I had tried to find the entrance–this was some years before the assault–but at first all my endeavours seemed in vain. The house was as forbidding as the outer appearance of the tower attached to it. And what was more, I could find no trace of a caretaker nor was I able to glean any information elsewhere. Weeks later, when I had put the whole matter out of my mind, giving it up as one of those unfulfilled dreams, quite by chance and in a completely different context, a lady was able to put me in touch with the present tenant of the Kornhäuselturm. We arranged a meeting and one morning two weeks later I was standing panting–after climbing four flights of stairs–in front of his door.

I find it so befitting that after more than 150 years the owner should again be an architect, someone who really appreciates this unique building. He has, on the one hand, left the basic tower as he found it, but on the other, has furnished it in a very modern style. Thus, much of the original atmosphere has been retained–yet there is nothing museum-like about the apartment. On the contrary, it must be great fun to live there. Let me try to describe it: in all, it has six storeys connected by narrow iron ladder-like staircases. Inside the front door is a vestibule as well as a bathroom, shower and toilet. On the second floor–this is where the original studio used to be–there is a light room with a vaulted ceiling, now once more used as a studio. Originally there used to be one more window, but this was walled up soon after Kornhäusel started to work there because the fantastic view distracted the apprentices from their tasks. The bedroom is also on this floor. The third storey contains a delightful little kitchen and dining area, while the fourth has a beautiful sitting room with four windows revealing a breath-taking view over Vienna. This is where you can also still see the remains of the drawbridge (see p. 68)–the staircase is similar to those you have just ascended, but at the bottom you can discern the place where a chain or rope must have been attached. Therefore, the opening on to the next floor is like a trap door and leads up to a room now used as a spare bedroom. Finally, from there you can climb up and out on to a flat roof. Again, and even more so–as the panorama spreads out on all sides–the view is phenomenal. It was at one time a normal sloping roof with a grid on top and it was from here that Adalbert Stifter, the writer, watched an eclipse of the sun which he has so expertly described. A plaque commemorating Stifter's stay in this house (Seitenstettengasse 2) can be found downstairs on the outer wall.

Further on down Seitenstettengasse, at No. 4, there is the second important building: the Jewish Synagogue. It, too, is a work of Kornhäusel's and in accordance with the prevailing regulations (no Jewish place of worship was allowed to be visible from the street), it is tucked away in the courtyard of the house. It has been on this site for over 150 years. Although damaged during the "Kristallnacht", the night of November 9, 1938 when the Nazis blew up most Jewish temples and synagogues, broke into shops and private homes, pillaging and burning, this synagogue was not completely demolished as it was located in the midst of other buildings which would also have been endangered.

We follow the street down to Rabensteig, turn right and almost immediately again left. Here we are in a kind of appendix to Rotenturmstrasse and, in spite of going into it at right angles, it is also called Rotenturmstrasse. For once, the Viennese seem to have run out of names for this short lane.

We cross over the main street and, bearing slightly to the left, find ourselves on Griechengasse.

Griechengasse

This lane is very ancient in its origin and upon entering it one becomes aware of a strangely medieval conglomeration of roofs at the other end. It is from this vantage point that you can get the best view of Vienna's oldest dwelling. This is a Gothic tower, originally one of the watchtowers of the old town wall, but later used as living quarters. Its angular roof appears in the oldest existing view of the city, which is part of the Babenberg family tree dated 1483 (exhibited at the Monastery of Klosterneuburg), only then it was still one of many such fortification towers.

No. 3 stands on the site of the "Küssdenpfennig-Haus"

(Kiss the Penny House). This house owed its name to the following legend: The innkeeper of the Black Eagle Inn was an avaricious man who loved money above everything else. One night very late, a stranger came to the inn. The innkeeper wanted to turn him away because he looked like some impecunious student, but the man promised to pay him well if he could stay the night. In fact he stayed on, day after day, and the innkeeper became very anxious about his rent. One day, unable to bear it any longer, he knocked at the man's door and demanded his money. "Here's a penny for you, for the time being. I'll pay the rest later," said the stranger, handing him a copper penny. The innkeeper flew into a rage, threw the penny on the floor and threatened to call the guard. The guest smiled and said: "I wouldn't throw that penny away, if I were you. It is worth a great deal." Bending down the innkeeper picked up the coin and found to his astonishment that it had turned to pure gold. "Now that's a penny I'll kiss," he cried, delighted to find it worth far more than the man owed him.

Soon the story of the golden coin spread and the inn was always full of people wanting to see the miraculous penny and to hear about the famous Doctor Paracelsus who had stayed at the inn and paid for his lodgings with it. (Theophrastus Bombastus von Hohenheim, known as Paracelsus, born 1493 in Switzerland, died 1541 in Salzburg. Physician, chemist, alchemist, he was reputed to have found a means of turning base metal into gold.) Naturally they stayed for a glass or two of wine and our innkeeper grew wealthy in the process. Thenceforth the house carried a sign showing a man kissing a golden penny and became known as the Küssdenpfennig-Haus. After such a delightful story it is somewhat a come down to have to admit that an old Viennese butcher's family by the name of Chussenphenninch can be traced back as far as 1360. This family owned a house–probably No. 3–"next to the Red Tower near the potters" and as of 1470 No. 3 bore the sign "Zum Kuechsenphennig".

We pass the Greek church on the left and then the lane widens to a kind of platform. Steps lead down towards

View of the Gothic Dwelling Tower

the Danube Canal. This area is called Hafnersteig (Potter's Stairs) and was the centre of the potter's trade. The locality in front of Griechengasse No. 7 was used as a gathering place for the City Militia when the alarm bell was sounded.

House No. 7, with its Madonna above the door, is a delightful building in its own right and though it bears the sign "House with Gothic Dwelling Tower", the tower is barely visible from the street. Even by entering the hall and looking out into the inner court you catch only a very disappointing glimpse of its lower part. But this entrance hall has other compensations, for one the pump well to the right of the door. Today it is no longer in use, but up to 1976 it still supplied some of the inhabitants with their water. Next to it on the wall are two lines of Arabic or possibly Persian writing. This has long been a puzzle to visitors and explanations as to how it got there and what it means range from the sublime to the obscene. An old woman, inmate of the house, claims that it has something to do with the Turks, some say it is a verse from the Koran, while others are convinced it is a bawdy rhyme.

Coming out of the house, Griechengasse continues to our left, though this last stretch is indeed very narrow. It must have posed traffic problems in days gone by, too, as the ancient stones set up to guard the house walls, confirm. Imprints of wheels trying to squeeze through this bottleneck can still be seen on them. Moreover, a proclamation dated May 8, 1902, on the house at the corner reads:

Pedestrians beware of traffic! Drive slowly! Coachmen with heavy vehicles must lead their horses or must send an adult escort ahead to warn pedestrians.

Another of those Viennese mysteries: When I began my research for this book some years ago, this notice bore the date 1912 and with this date I had included it. In 1986, while updating my material, I went by there and found to my surprise that someone had very meticulously changed the second one to a zero, so that the date now reads 1902. I spent a great deal of time trying to locate

Griechengasse

someone who could explain why this was done and who had done it. It looks too neat for vandalism, apart from the fact that it would be rather difficult to attach without attracting notice. So far none of the offices possibly responsible knew anything about it.

No. 9 at the corner is part of the famous Griechenbeisl (see Fleischmarkt). The Greeks, to which both the street and the restaurant refer, did not frequent this region until the 18th century.

Now let us walk to the end of this truly medieval lane to Fleischmarkt.

Fleischmarkt

This ancient street is first mentioned in the records about 1220. The butchers had their Guildhall here and in the late Middle Ages it was a refined district where the rich members of this trade had their homes.

Immediately to our left is the "Griechenbeisl" restaurant. Prior to its present name it was known by various appellations. At one time it was called "The Red Roof", at another "The Golden Angel" and for a while "The Yellow Eagle". It is one of the oldest restaurants in Vienna, its origins dating back to 1500. On entering the hall you can see the history of the house on the right and, on the left, where a staircase leads up to the first floor, three cannon balls are protruding from the wall. The text beside them reads:

In the year 1529 the Yellow Eagle Inn stood where the Griechenbeisl now stands and was part of the town fortifications of Vienna and a bastion against the oncoming Turks, it stood in the direct line of fire of their cannon. During the restoration of the house in 1963 these three cannon balls were found and confirm the illustrious past of our house.

In the days when it was known as "The Red Roof" the Great Plague swept through Vienna. It was by no means the first time that such an epidemic decimated the population; there had been three major plague years: 1349, 1364 and 1679. There was little anyone could do. Mostly, no doubt, the sanitary conditions were to blame. But the cures thought up by physicians hardly helped matters as the following excerpt shows:

"When the swelling grows or causes pain, he shall soak a toad that has been skewered through the head (not through the belly) in summer . . . which shall be laid with its belly against the plague boil so as to draw out the poison, however, it were better if this toad were ground to powder and mixed with yellow wax to make a plaster and to apply it because this could be used not only for one but for many sick men." (Cure for the Plague, by Dr. Sorbait, the famous Plague Doctor, 1679; see also p. 68).

It is said that during the last outburst of the plague there lived a bagpiper and singer by the name of Augustin. He used to make a living by going from tavern to tavern, singing and playing his bagpipes. He was obviously popular, because everyone referred to him as "dear" Augustin and he was not averse to accepting a glass or two of wine as a token of his audience's appreciation.

In 1679 people were dying like flies and no sooner had they breathed their last than they were thrown on to the street and carted away for burial in order to avoid infecting the survivors. But as they died by the hundreds there was no time or money to give each of them a decent burial with a grave of his own. Every night the deathcart would roll through the streets of the city and the corpses lying on the pavement were heaved on to it. With this gruesome load, the cart was driven out of the city limits and the bodies thrown into a large pit where they were then covered with quicklime.

The inhabitants of the stricken city sought diversion by frequenting the wine houses even more avidly than ever in order to find a few hours of gaiety and oblivion. Augustin was in his element. He sang, played and drank with the best of them.

One night he had drunk rather too heavily and when he stumbled out into the street in the early hours of the morning, his legs buckled under him and down he went into the gutter where he slept the deep sleep of the very drunk.

A little while later the deathcart came by and the two men, taking him for just another corpse, picked him up gingerly with their long poles and hoisted him on to the cart. Augustin, in his stupor, did not even stir.

When the cart reached its destination, the two men emptied their gruesome load into the waiting pit, but being tired they decided to leave the quicklime till later and went off.

It was well into the afternoon before Augustin came to and looked around. For a while he could not figure it out. When he finally realized, where he was, he began to curse and call for help. But no one came to his aid because no one heard him. Augustin, in desperation, pulled and tugged at his bagpipes until they were free of the bodies around him and began to play for all he was worth. And sure enough, people heard him and recognized that unmistakable Augustin tune.

> "O du lieber Augustin, Augustin, Augustin,
> O du lieber Augustin, alles ist hin."
> (O dear Augustin, Augustin, Augustin,
> O dear Augustin, everything's gone.)

They ran to the edge of the pit, threw down a rope and pulled him out.

It was no doubt a miracle that he was found before the grave-diggers put the quicklime on the corpses, but it was certainly an even greater miracle that, despite his close contact with pestilence-stricken bodies, Augustin did not get the plague but lived to tell the story for many years to come.

Directly across from the Griechenbeisel, on house No. 18, up on the third floor of the facade there is a relief of Emperor Joseph II with a rather stilted rhyme which claims that "this house may be transitory, but not so Joseph's fame; he gave us tolerance which gives him immortality,"–a touching token of gratitude.

Turning away from the Griechenbeisel, past the Greek Orthodox Church, we cross to the other side of the street. We pass Wolfengasse, named after a tavern once situated there, called "The White Wolf" and almost immediately come to another street named after as fearsome a creature, "Drachengasse". This "dragon", how-

ever, was not as terrifying as it sounds; the name refers
to one Johann Martin Drach, a City Counsellor of the
year 1660 whose house understandably bore the sign of a
dragon.

We then turn sharply to the right into Postgasse and so
reach Schönlaterngasse.

Otto Wagner's Postsparkasse

If you are interested in the architecture of the turn of the
century, you may at this point wish to make a small detour to include a famous Otto Wagner building: the
Postsparkasse (Postal Savings Bank). If not, skip the next
page and go straight on to Schönlaterngasse.

It is a little complicated to get to the Postsparkasse: from
Fleischmarkt you turn left into Postgasse, walk down it
as far as Auwinkel; from here to the right until you reach
Dominikanerbastei. Crossing it, the next street to your
left is Wiesingerstrasse and here we are already walking
along one side of the Postal Savings Bank which takes up
an entire block.

Built between 1904–1912, it is one of the best examples
of a carefully planned, functional office building. Even
here you can already admire one of the sensational inno-
vations that Otto Wagner applied: he used thin marble
panels for the facade and these were attached by metal
bolts which simultaneously become a new kind of dec-
orative element. But Wagner also used another at that
time unusual material for his ornaments, namely aluminium. In both cases his choice of materials illustrates very
clearly that a simple and economical structure can still be
beautiful.

At the next corner (Biberstrasse) you turn right and
shortly find yourself on Cochplatz in front of the main
entrance to the bank.

After having paid your tribute to this prototype of mod-

Otto Wagner's Postal Savings Bank

ern architecture, turn around for a minute and look towards the Ring where the ostentatious erstwhile War Ministry (now Ministry of Agriculture, Construction etc.) stands; built almost at the same time, it is still completely under the influence of the Historicism which characterizes the Ringstrasse. Comparing the two buildings, you get some kind of idea how far out Wagner's concepts must have seemed to his contemporaries.

Should the bank be open, I would suggest that you go in, for Wagner was also responsible for the interior decoration. Much of this is still there, such as the aluminium hot-air blowers in the large main hall. This hall is unique in its functional simplicity and elegance.

Outside once again, we turn right and walk around the building to Rosenbursengasse, cross Dominikanerbastei and up Barbaragasse. Here, too, it is interesting to compare the architecture we have just seen with the rather pompous turn of the century houses along the way.

Barbaragasse leads us back to Postgasse where we turn right and almost immediately left again, bringing us to Schönlaterngasse.

Schönlaterngasse

The name is due to a beautiful lantern, a copy of which still graces No. 6; the original is in the Historical Museum of the City.

The street begins on a macabre note: the first house on the right, No. 13, is known as the "Totendoktorhaus" (the Death Doctor's House). In the 15th century one of the chancellors of the nearby University, Paul Urssenbeck, made it his home. He is supposed to have been the greatest diagnostician of his era, in fact people suspected him of being in league with the devil because of it. This suspicion was further fed when he was able to save the life of Count Auersperg, who had already been given up for dead. And when Urssenbeck himself died shortly after, it was whispered abroad that he had forfeited his life for that of the Count.

No. 9 is the home of both the restaurant and the literary club "Die Alte Schmiede" (The Old Forge). In fact, it contains a complete smithy, forge, anvil, blowers, hammers, nails and all which can be seen through the window.

Its neighbour, No. 7, is the famous Basiliskenhaus where a horrible monster was discovered in the well in 1212. The legend even refers to the exact date: the morning of

Schönlaterngasse

June 26. A baker lived here and it was his apprentice boy who noticed a foul smell coming from the well. A learned man in the crowd that soon gathered in the street declared that a creature was sitting at the bottom and that it was the feared basilisk, a cross between a toad and a cock. The baker's boy volunteered to climb down but, afraid of looking at this creature, he took care to take a mirror with him. With this he confronted the monster and on seeing its own image the creature turned to stone. The result can still be seen high up on the facade of the building, where a strangely shaped stone is set in a niche. There is also a painting which represents the apprentice's courageous deed.

Across the street at No. 6 is the beautiful lantern at No. 6

and at No. 4 you can admire a lovely bay window. This, and the adjoining windows of that house, at one time showed many a pretty damsel freely displaying her charms as the beautiful lantern glowed in a reddish light at this end of the street.

Heiligenkreuzerhof

A large green, wooden doorway leads from Schönlaterngasse into a wide court–a world of its own, shut off from the city. The buildings surrounding it are Vienna's oldest tenement houses and have belonged to the Cistercian Monastery at Heiligenkreuz (south of Vienna) since the first half of the 13th century. But their foundations are even older, for the cellars have vaulting that presumably goes back to 1170.

In the courtyard, a small portion of the roughcast of the wall has been scraped away to reveal part of another wall from the time of the Babenberg Dukes as the plaque next to it informs us.

The houses, as they now stand, date from the middle of the 17th and early 18th centuries. The lovely little St. Bernhard's Chapel incorporated into this complex features an altar painting by Martin Altomonte and, in general, is a gem of a Baroque interior. Unfortunately, it is usually closed, except when very elite weddings are held there. The Hauswart (caretaker) lives at the other end of the courtyard, he is usually willing to let you see the chapel and perhaps even the ancient vaults. But as he is under no obligation to do so, a small token of your gratitude would be appreciated.

There is also the lovely stone lintel over the entrance leading to the prelate's garden under which at one time there was no doubt an elaborate wrought-iron gate. It lends itself well as a backdrop for theatre performances and has, time and again, been used as such. Moreover, the Vienna Boys' Choir give their annual open-air concert at the opening of the Vienna Festival on a podium set up in front of it.

Sonnenfelsgasse

Having left the Heiligenkreuzerhof by the far exit, which leads into Grashofgasse–a building by the name of "Grashof" can be traced back to 1337–we reach Köllnerhofgasse after only a few steps and here we turn left. Köllnerhofgasse was once the centre of trade for rich merchants from the Rhine and is mentioned as early as the 13th century as the site of a large inn frequented by tradesmen from Cologne.

Köllnerhofgasse runs into Sonnenfelsgasse, named after one of Maria Theresa's counsellors, a lawyer, writer and scholar. He also brought about the abolition of torture and was certainly one of the most enlightened men of his age. Because Sonnenfels was a Jew, the street's name was changed under the Nazi regime and for a while was called Johann-Sebastian-Bach-Gasse, but reverted to its former appellation in 1945.

Almost immediately, at No. 3, we encounter one of the most lovely houses in town, known as the "Hildebrandthaus". The house itself is 14th or 15th century, but was rebuilt in 1721 with a facade in the style of Johann Lukas von Hildebrandt. One of Vienna's well-known wine cellars, the "Zwölfapostelkeller" (Twelve Apostles' Cellar) is located here.

Further down the street (No. 19) is the old "Domus Universitatis", the erstwhile University administration building, for here we are only a few steps from the site of the old University. This building also housed the student jail, as well as the University archives and has a pretty roofed-in courtyard, which you should not miss.

Dr.-Ignaz-Seipel-Platz

And here we are right in the centre of the academic world of days gone by. Across the square stood the Old University–the second oldest in Central Europe–founded by Rudolph IV in 1365. The building now on that historic site was built in the 1620's by the Jesuits and it is their church that commands the entire square. After the University had moved to its new building across the way (the Academy of Sciences), the old house was, for a while, used by the Vienna Boys' Choir and Schubert spent some time there as a student and chorister. The reason for his rather premature departure was due to an incorrigible dislike of mathematics.

Prior to the great Jesuit counter-reformation, there was a student dormitory where the church now stands. It was called "Bursa agni" and the house sign showed a gentle lamb which caused malicious tongues to call the dormitory "the house with the misleading name", for the students living there had a reputation of being anything but gentle lambs. The students in those days had altogether a rather tainted reputation it seems: "Moreover, the students devote themselves entirely to pleasure and think of nothing but wine and good food. Only few of them become scholars and they are very hard to keep in check. Day and night they go marauding through the city and are a veritable pest to the citizens. What is more, the women's desirability distracts them" (Extract from a letter which Aeneas Silvius Piccolomini wrote in 1438).

The Jesuits pulled down the "Bursa" and five more houses to make way for their magnificent church. Even though the University was transferred to its new location on the Ring in 1884, the church is still often referred to as the University Church. Do go in for a moment and admire the barley-sugar spiral columns, as well as the trompe l'oeil cupola. There is a stone of a lighter colour than the rest in the centre aisle and if you stand there and look up at the ceiling it does, indeed, look like a dome.

Opposite the Old University is the Academy of Sciences, originally built to supplement the University, which could no longer house all its students. This building contains a hall whose beautiful painted ceiling was badly damaged by fire in 1961, but has since been restored. The hall is still used for festive academic events. It was here that Haydn witnessed a performance of his "Creation". Already a very old man at the time, it was to be his last public appearance. Among those who thronged to congratulate him after the performance, there was a stocky young man with a rather unruly head of hair, who went down on his knees and reverently kissed the aged maestro's hand. Haydn is said to have laid one hand on young Beethoven's head and said: "You will finish, what I began."

The square has something theatrical about it and the Jesuits did indeed use it as a setting for open-air plays. In recent years this tradition was reactivated for the performance of a medieval morality play and it is a pity this is not done more often. However, every summer this splendid Baroque church is the site of the "Spectacvlvm", a programme of baroque church operas and modern biblical ballets.

Bäckerstrasse

On the other side of the Academy of Sciences we enter Bäckerstrasse, at one time no doubt the bakers' street though no specific facts are known to prove this. The first house on your left was once what would correspond to a student cafeteria (No. 16). It was a certain Barbara Roman who first had the brilliant idea of asking for leftovers from the imperial kitchens and selling them cheaply, to students. Others quickly followed her example, but by far the most famous of such establishments, which went by the name of "Schmauswaberl"–Waberl being a diminutive of Barbara–was the one at No. 16 Bäckerstrasse. Today the house shows no traces of its "illustri-

The cow playing checkers

ous" past, but is nevertheless a fine example of a well-to-do citizen's home from the beginning of the 18th century.

A recent discovery is the delightful house-sign which came to light when No. 12 was being restored. "Where the cow is playing checkers" was the name of this building. You can see a bespectacled cow with a chess-board (backgammon to be exact) and, as her partner in the game, a wolf. Unfortunately the porch, obviously added later, has swallowed up most of the wolf: you can only just see its snout.

Originally, this sign must have been rather more elaborate as a detailed description of it speaks of a fox and not a wolf. There presumably must have been more than one house with this or a similar sign, for mention of one is made on Wallnerstrasse. But here is how the Viennese saw the sign back in the 17th and 18th centuries:

The whole thing was like a comic strip. The fox (or wolf) is saying to the cow: "When I throw my dice, your skin will be mine", and the cow answers: "Stop boasting, you'll soon be in poor shape yourself!" Between them is a tanner, wielding a fly-swatter. "I'm biding my time to see who'll win," says he. The description also mentions a hunter and his dog, none of which are visible in today's remnants. But the fly next to the cow's head can still be seen plainly.

There is more to this seemingly harmless fable than meets the eye: it is an ironic comment on the struggle between the Protestants and the Catholics in the 17th century. The cow represents the Catholics, the fox (or wolf) the Protestants, whereas the tanner, the hunter and his dog symbolize the greedy town counsellors and lawyers, while the fly stands for the rather helpless clergy.

Further up the street a small lane branches off to the right: Windhaaggasse. It is named after Enzmüller, Baron Windhaag, a prominent figure in the Counter-Reformation. He is said to have personally converted no less than 40,000 Protestants. But the members of this faith had little reason to love him and spread a gruesome story, proving his lack of humane emotions. His mother, Katharina, so they claimed, had once been walking across a deserted cemetery in the middle of the night when suddenly a skeleton jumped on her back and forced her to carry it piggy-back to her house (No. 9). There it disappeared, but nine months later she gave birth to Enzmüller. There is a Catholic version of this tale which confirms that Katharina did indeed carry a skeleton piggy-back, but the courageous woman did it to put a hauted soul at rest. Be that as it may, No. 9 used to be called the "Piggy-Back House". It was here that Windhaag's Foundation for Alumnis was located. In 1944, a bomb destroyed the old house, leaving only the facade standing; but it has since been restored.

We now come to what I consider is perhaps *the* most charming courtyard in Vienna. It is at No. 7, and has the best preserved Renaissance courtyard in town, particularly lovely when the abundance of creeper surrounds the statue of the Madonna which looks down upon this old-world enchantment. There, on the right, is the old stable where horses were given water and fodder. It conjures up vivid scenes of life in the 16th century–a life so very far removed from our own. The open galleries above have, in part, been walled up. On the walls of the first floor balcony there is a unique display of fine wrought-iron decorations which come from the collection of the Biedermeier painter Friedrich Amerling.

Here is a spot where one is tempted to linger–but as there is still so much to see, let us bid farewell to this island of tranquillity and proceed towards Lugeck.

Lugeck

At the corner of Bäckerstrasse and Lugeck stood the famous Regensburgerhof, the inn where merchants from Bavaria would take lodging while in Vienna. It was destroyed in the late 19th century, but the architect who built the present building on its site has tried to adhere to the historically characteristic style of its predecessor. Over the doorway of Bäckerstrasse No. 1 there is an inscription commemorating its past:

"On this site stood the old Regensburgerhof, once the residence of Bavarian merchants. Here the Viennese citizen, Niklas Teschler, was host to Emperor Frederick III and King Matthias Corvinus in 1470. In this same house, Emperor Joseph I installed the Public Imperial Pawn Office."

First mentioned in 1275, the name Lugeck may have referred to a Lug-ins-Land (a watch-tower), though no proof of the existence of such a tower has so far been found.

Where the statue of Gutenberg now stands, there was once a large hole. It appears on Hirschvogel's map of Vienna dated 1547, under the name of "Marcus Curtius Loch". Marcus Curtius was a Roman hero who cast himself into a chasm which had suddenly appeared in the middle of the Roman Forum. By his voluntary death he averted great danger threatening the State. To this day archeologists are puzzled as to what purpose this hole served. The following explanations have been put forward: it might have been a) a well, b) a bell foundry pit, c) an air vent leading to the catacombs, d) a place of execution or e) a place of sanctuary. There is even one version that claims the whole thing was a student joke and served no purpose at all.

Proceeding towards Rotenturmstrasse we come to No. 6 which is known as the Federlhof. It was once one of Vienna's most elaborate mansions and in 1591, was owned by a merchant, one Georg Federl, hence the name. Legend claims that Philippine Welser stayed here. She was the daughter of a famous German banker and married Archduke Ferdinand (1557)–an unheard of misalliance in those days; as a result his heirs lost the right of succession. The house is said to have had several other illustrious guests, among them Paracelsus, Wallenstein and Leibnitz. On the walls inside the door are remnants of the Renaissance portal and a 17th century relief depicting the Virgin Mary.

Back to Bäckerstrasse, Lugeck No. 5 leads into a court, the other end of which opens on to Wollzeile No. 5. This court bears a strange name: Schmeckender Wurmhof–the Court of the Smelling Worm (Schmecken in Viennese dialect means to smell or to savour). Again there are two versions of the explanation of this unusual appellation. The first, and obviously much older of the two, claims that a dragon–or "worm" as the Viennese called it–was found in a cellar of one of the surrounding houses. It exuded a most horrible stench and what would be more natural than to name the adjoining court after "the smelling worm".

The second story is far more charming. Towards the end of the 17th century one of the houses belonged to a purse-maker, one Schmiedhuber, who had a beautiful daughter with the rather extravagant name of Salome. Schmiedhuber lived over his purse and bag shop and had an alligator hanging over the doorway as the sign of his trade.

A young student, deeply in love with pretty Salome, stood one night beneath her window, hoping to catch a glimpse of his beloved. For a long time Salome let him wait, but when she finally graciously leaned out, he threw a bunch of wild flowers up to her. The cruel girl disdained to catch it and the flowers fell, right between the paws of the alligator, where they stayed.

Next morning, passing citizens laughed to see this outlandish "worm" seemingly intent on smelling the fragrant bunch between its claws.

If you now walk through the court, you will come on to Wollzeile and, crossing the street, you enter yet another such passageway, which leads you back to St. Stephen's.

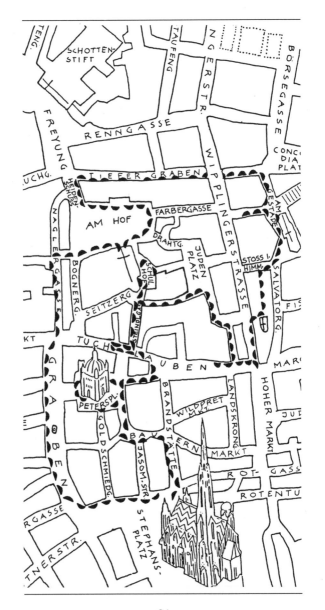

FOURTH TOUR

Brandstätte

It is easiest to start off again from St. Stepen's Main Gate. Across from it, on the other side of the square is Jasomirgottstrasse. A strange name that, for a street: "Yes, so God". It refers to the Babenberg Duke Henry II, who was given this nickname because he was constantly using the expression "Ja, so mir Gott helfe". (Yes, so help me God.) We won't enter it, though, but turn right until we arrive at Brandstätte.

Your first guess would probably be that this area must at one time have been laid waste by a fire. Historians presume it to have been the great holocausts which devastated the city in 1276 or 1327. No matter, the street has meanwhile fully earned its name from the ravaging flames that engulfed it in April 1945.

Until well into the 15th century the place was an open area and tournaments used to be held here every year on Shrove Tuesday. The rest of the time some booths selling market produce and others belonging to moneylenders stood here.

We follow the street as far as Bauernmarkt. Before turning left here, do look at the large building (Brandstätte No. 6) on the right with the enormous figure of the archangel Michael on the front. It is the Zacherlhaus, built by Josef Plecnik, one of Otto Wagner's students; the sculpture is by Ferdinand Andri, a member of the Secession.

Bauernmarkt

This was the farmers' market, a market selling agricultural produce right up to the 18th century. At one time it also went by the name "Hen's Lookout" due to the poultry on sale there. Another speciality which seems to have been extremely popular–strange as it may sound–was stale bread and cakes.

St. John Nepomuk

We turn left into Bauernmarkt.

Do go into the pleasant courtyard of No. 1 (just before
we reach Freisingergasse), where there is a statue of
St. Johann Nepomuk. He is a saint little known in
Anglo-Saxon countries, but in this part of the world
Nepomuk is the patron saint of bridges because King

Wenceslas (certainly not "good" King Wenceslas!) had him thrown into the River Moldava from a bridge in Prague. Legend claims that Nepomuk was the Queen's confessor and Wenceslas wanted him to divulge her confessional secrets. Nepomuk refused. According to recent research, he never was the Queen's confessor, but he did have a quarrel with Wenceslas concerning ecclesiastic matters and Wenceslas, a notorious dipsomaniac much given to outbursts of fury, had him tortured and thrown into the river.

If you look closer, you will see that the good saint is standing on a delightful little devil who is sticking two fingers into his mouth. Whether this gesture is one of coyness or whether the mischievous rascal is about to let forth a shrill whistle, I do not know. But he is supposed to be a personification of the River Moldava.

We return to Bauernmarkt, turn right, and so around the corner into Freisingergasse.

Freisingergasse

The street name refers to Bishop Otto von Freising who built a large house at the corner of Graben in the middle of the 12th century. The corner house of Bauernmarkt and Freisingergasse (No. 4) belonged to the mighty imperial Court Jew, Samuel Oppenheimer. He was Leopold I's court banker and financier of Prince Eugene's military campaigns. He also possessed of a rare and very valuable library which was bought and incorporated into the Bodleyan Library in Oxford in 1829. This was the site of a terrible tragedy: the utter ruin of a wealthy man through no fault of his own.

It all started on July 22, 1700, when two chimney-sweeps–Italians, as were most of the members of this profession at that time–were sitting in front of the "Chimney-Sweep" beer tavern, playing a game of "alla mora".

In the course of the game, they gesticulated very excitedly and Oppenheimer's doorman, who was watching from across the road, couldn't help laughing. The two Italians were offended and a heated discussion ensued.

Very soon apprentices and other spectators gathered and before long there was quite a crowd. The majority took the side of the chimney-sweeps, openly voicing their dislike of Jews in general. Eggs were brought from the near-by market and Oppenheimer's windows bombarded. The crowd got more and more incensed and before the town militia could intervene, the mob had forced the main gate, invaded the living quarters and stock rooms and started looting. Books, silverware and goods of every kind were thrown into the street. When the guards finally arrived, they had to use their weapons to disperse the rabble. There was quite a bit of shooting and not a few casualties. That evening a new uproar started and could only be put down after Prince Eugene gave orders for the big cannon to be set up in front of the Oppenheimer residence.

The ringleaders were arrested and hanged from the very house they had destroyed.

But Oppenheimer had lost over a hundred thousand Guilders within one day. This affair so shook his reputation that he became bankrupt. His bankruptcy, however, was to affect Vienna's entire economy for many years to come.

There is a relief of the Annunciation on the facade of this building. It is the first memorial in Vienna to the pestilence asking the Virgin to "spare us from the plague".

Petersplatz

As already mentioned this, too, was once a market place. The poet Wolfgang Schmelzl (1548) lists the following produce on sale there:

eggs, chickens, hens, geese, ducks, fat capons, beetroots, turnips, horse-radish, cabbage, parsley and lettuce. At the time of the two Turkish sieges, when food was getting scarce in the city, you could buy larded "roof hares", as cats were euphemistically called, but only the richest citizens could afford such a luxury.

What is more, this was the seat of the city oil supplier, who sold oil for the lamps which constituted the city's illumination. In 1688, a decree was issued that house owners had to fill the lanterns daily which the municipality had put at their disposal. "He who shall maliciously destroy such lamps as have been put up in many places, whoever he may be, shall forfeit his right hand" (Decree issued by Leopold I). Up to 1561, every citizen out after dark had to carry his own light, usually a lantern. But the aristocracy employed boys to run ahead bearing links or torches. The Emperor Ferdinand I decreed that no one be allowed to walk abroad without a light once the Beer Bell at St. Stephen's had been rung. The Beer Bell, also referred to as the "Throatcutter", was so called because when it rang all beer and wine houses had to close down, the "time, gentlemen, please", of those days.

Let us first walk round the back of the church. No. 10 is a rather lovely old house. At one time it bore the sign "The Peasants' Dance" and was a gruesome reminder of the Peasant Revolt of 1595. The ringleaders were beheaded at Am Hof nearby and many other participants had their ears and noses cut off. This gave the owner of the house the idea for his sign, which showed the mutilated peasants performing a horrible dance. In this same house, where there is now a ladies' fashion shop, there used to be a baker. He was called "Peter's Baker" (St. Peter's being right opposite) and young Mozart bought his "Kipfels" there and even praised them in one of his letters. The bakery business was carried on in this house for two centuries right up to 1967, when the last bakery was closed down.

Next door is the Hotel Wandl, once Hotel Daum. The latter opened in 1851, with every imaginable luxury and in accordance with the latest Parisian style. On the day of its opening the Viennese–some 47,000 of them–could for a small fee visit the hotel and satisfy their curiosity. Three years later Johann Wandl bought it and added an elevator and bathrooms. It had the reputation of being one of the most elegant European hotels of its time.

We keep left along the side of the church until we reach the front entrance. It is likely that a temple stood here during the Roman occupation, but it is also supposed to be the oldest Christian place of worship in Vienna. Certainly its foundations are older than St. Stephen's or St. Ruprecht's. Legend has it that Charlemagne founded it in 792 and the large relief on the south-east wall of the church depicts this event.

Inside St. Peter's, to the left of the doorway, there is Wolfgang Lazius' epitaph (see Lazenhof p. 68). The present building being relatively new–for Vienna–there do not seem to be any particular legends connected with it. Should you be visiting at Christmas-time, do go and see the exhibition of crèches in the crypt.

Jungferngasse

Leading from the front entrance of the church to Graben is a very short street–if one can call it a street at all, for it cannot even boast of a single house entrance–and, at one time, it was also one of the narrowest. It is called Jungferngässel (Virgin Lane). This name has given rise to speculation with some saying it is short for "frivolous virgin's lane" in connection with the legend that follows. Others claim that, due to its lack of entrances, it is unapproachable like a virgin.

At one time, before it was widened, this little alley was spanned by arches. On one side lived a maiden by the name of Frowiza, while across the way was the home of the City Counsellor Stephan Knogler. Mr. Knogler had a son who was much taken with pretty Frowiza and at night he used to climb over the arches to see his love. One night he was once again making his precarious journey over the arches when his father caught sight of him and called out angrily. The poor boy got such a fright that, losing his footing, he fell and broke his neck.

At the corner of Graben (No. 21) there was once a house sporting a most unusual sign: "The Dog in the Basket". The story goes that when Frederick III was besieged in the Hofburg (Town Palace) in 1462 and food had become very scarce, a tailor by the name of Kronberger took it upon himself to come to the rescue. He prepared a basket of food, concealed himself in it and had them pull him up to a window over the moat. When the guards became suspicious, the ingenious tailor began to bark like a dog. This fooled the soldiers and they let the basket go up, thinking that if the occupants of the palace were already so hard pressed that they had to resort to dog's meat, the siege would surely soon be over.

After the revolt was suppressed, the Emperor gave Kronberger a house which henceforth proudly bore the name "Zum Hund im Korb" (The Dog in the Basket).

Kühfussgasse

We return to the back of the church of St. Peter's from where, next to the Hotel Wandl, a narrow lane leads off at an angle: Kühfussgasse. A beer tavern is responsible for the name; it had a house sign which read:

> O Mensch, thue Buss,
> Denn hier ist der Kühfuss.

which translated is just as cryptic–"O man repent, for here is the cow's foot". I am afraid this verse will have to remain a mystery, for to this day no one has been able to find out to what it refers.

At the other end, we come out into Tuchlauben.

Tuchlauben (1)

As early as the 13th century arcades lined this street, which was the centre of the cloth trade.

At the point where we enter, there is a statue of a cloth merchant in the centre of a kind of triangle, caused, it seems, by a widening of the street. This unusual shape has led archeologists to presume that it was the site of Vienna's first market place, older even than Hoher Markt; similarly shaped markets in other Austrian towns are all dated prior to 1000 A.D.

Keeping left, we cross the road to where a large handsome store selling linen, towels, etc. stands at the corner. The name is Gunkel & Co. and that name takes us back to 1796, when Joseph Gunkel opened his shop (originally over on Graben) and became one of Europe's most famous tailors. He even features in one of Johann Nestroy's plays. The present shop was founded in 1837 and on entering you will find its history written up just inside the door.

We pursue Tuchlauben, still keeping left, until we reach No. 5, the Hochholzerhof. Recently restored, this 17th century building once again features the arcades (Lauben) which gave the street its name. When the bombing of Vienna started in 1945 the Virgin on the facade was taken down and stored in the cellar of the Augustinian Friars Monastery. Even there it was not really safe, for the cellar was badly hit, but luckily the statue remained unharmed. The name of the building goes back to a butcher by the name of Leonhard Hochholzer who owned the original house in 1555; the present one was built in the 17th century, while the facade is dated 1719.

Retracing our steps to the corner of Steindlgasse, we are about to branch off for a while, but will return to Tuchlauben at its further end a little later.

Steindlgasse

This street is very pretty and rather surprising. At its end the Gothic choir of the Church Am Hof juts out into the roadway and to the right there are the lanterns of the "Gösser Bierklinik", which is no doubt the most prominent feature of the street. This restaurant is known by several names, "Bierklinik" being only one of them. It also goes under the name of a) Steindlwirt, b) Stiedl's, or c) Zum Goldenen Drachen. The original "Golden Dragon", which at one time was the house sign, can still be seen above the doorway behind glass. Inside the entrance on the left there is a short history of the restaurant, which is one of the oldest in Vienna (1566). The street itself is named after one of its owners, Johann Steindl, who received the restaurant as a reward for his bravery during the Turkish Siege.

The house was badly damaged in the last days of the war in 1945, but it also has the distinction of having been the first to be restored to its former appearance.

The house next door, No. 6, used to be called "The Golden Snake" and in 1451 it belonged to a most remarkable woman. This was Helene Kottanerin, a lady-in-waiting to Queen Elisabeth, the widow of Duke Albrecht V and mother of Ladislaus Postumus.

Elisabeth was in the last months of pregnancy when her husband died. She wanted to be sure that her child would be crowned with the Hungarian St. Stephen's crown and sent her lady-in-waiting with instructions to steal it from the fortress where it was kept.

Steindlgasse

This woman not only performed an unheard of feat, but–equally unheard of in those days–wrote a detailed account of her adventures.

This document is unique and it is worth quoting some excerpts from it. The original is written in the quaint spelling and language of the time, but reads like any modern thriller.

"When we arrived at the Plintenburg, the maidens were

delighted that they were to go to my Gracious Lady, got themselves ready and had a chest made for their clothes. And he who was with me also came into the women's room and joked with the maidens.

Now there was a pile of wood by the fireplace for making a fire and under this he hid the file. But the pages who served the maidens saw it under the wood and began to whisper to each other. This I heard and told him. Then he grew very agitated and took it away again, hiding it elsewhere. And he said to me: 'Woman, see to it that we have a light' and I asked an old woman to give me several candles because I needed to pray a lot. And when the maidens and everyone were asleep, I stayed in the small parlour and the old woman I had brought with me lay there fast asleep.

This was the right time and he who was in these difficulties with me came through the chapel to the door and knocked, whereupon I opened and locked it again after him.

Now he had brought a servant with him who had been sworn to secrecy and gave him the lock which was to be put back later and also gave him my Gracious Lady's little seal in order that it could be re-sealed and gave me the three keys, too, which fitted the outer door. Then he took off the cloth with the seal which the lord of the castle had put over the lock and unlocked it and entered. He worked hard at the other lock so that the knocking and filing was very loud and the master's retainers were very much awake that night, but God the Almighty had stopped up their ears and none of them heard him. And I prayed to God and while I was praying there was a great noise and banging as if many people in armour were at the gate. So I got up and wanted to warn them to stop working.

It then occurred to me to go to the gate, which I did, and when I got to the door there was no more banging and nothing to be heard and I vowed to Our Lady that I would make a pilgrimage barefoot to Zell and that until such time as I had taken it, I vowed not to lie in a featherbed on a Saturday night.

Just then he came towards me and bade me be cheerful, they had filed the lock off the door. But on the last door the lock was so fast that it could not be filed away. It would have to be broken open. This made a great deal of noise and I was afraid someone would ask what it was. Now that the Holy Crown was completely free, we closed all the doors again and put other locks in place of the locks that had been broken and placed My Lady's seal on them and locked the outer door again and covered it with the cloth and the seal again, just as we had found it. And I threw the file down the privy in the maidens' chamber. And the Holy Crown was carried out through the chapel. My helper then took a red velvet cushion, took the stitching out of it and put the Holy Crown inside the cushion and sewed it up again. By then it was almost day.

When the maidens and the servants were ready to leave, he who was with me took the cushion in which the Holy Crown was hidden and instructed his servant who had helped me, to carry the cushion out of the house to the sleigh. And the good boy took the cushion on his shoulder and an old cow hide as well, which had a long tail that trailed after him and we began to laugh . . ."

One can just imagine after the strain of that long night how their laughter brought release. But that wasn't the end of their adventures. They travelled across the wintry landscape in the dark until they came to the Danube which was frozen over, but in some places the ice was rather thin. Nevertheless, they tried to cross to the other side, but when they were in the middle one of their sleighs broke through the ice. Luckily, however, no one was drowned and though many of their belongings went under, the St. Stephen's Crown was saved and carried in triumph to Queen Elisabeth at Komorn. The Queen gave birth to a son, Ladislaus Postumus, and when he was only twelve weeks old the child was crowned with the St. Stephen's Crown.

Later, when Queen Elisabeth came to Vienna, she had to pawn this same crown in order to pay her retinue. Recently the crown was in the news again. American soldiers had taken it to the United States in 1945, where it was kept at Fort Knox until 1978. On January 5 of that year, it was returned to Budapest after much negotiation and handed over to the Hungarian people in a festive ceremony.

At the end of the street, where the church choir juts out, a narrow lane on the right leads to Schulhof.

Schulhof

This is where the Carmelite Monks had their cemetery and later, the Jesuits a school. Possibly the name refers to this school, though it might also be due to reminiscences of the nearby Judenplatz which, when it was still the centre of the Jewish community, went by the name of Schulhof, as the synagogue was located there (Yiddish for synagogue = shul).

Today, the small square is overshadowed by the Gothic choir of the Church Am Hof. As we enter, there is a tiny house tucked on to the side of the church which belongs to the watchmaker across the way. To the right are remnants of the same forbidding shutters we also encountered on Judengasse (see p. 66), even though this house was not part of the Jewish ghetto. Next to the shutters is the entrance to a small museum housing an amazing collection of old clocks which is well worth a visit. The exhibition takes up three storeys of this narrow little house and includes such rareties as the works of tower clocks from the 16th century a spit roast timer and the prettiest ladies' watches.

Next door, at No. 4, we find another of those pretty courts, as well as an interesting staircase. Even though you can reach Judenplatz via Parisergasse, I suggest you retrace your steps to Steindlgasse and take Kurrentgasse instead. It is far more rewarding.

Kurrentgasse

The Kottanerin house on Steindlgasse is also Kurrentgasse No. 2 which is the house in which St. Stanislaus
Kostka lived from 1564–1567. He was still a very young
boy at the time and a staunch Catholic. One day he fell
ill and asked for a priest. However, his landlord, one Caspar Wachenschwanz, a tailor and a Protestant, refused
his request. That night Kostka had a vision of St. Barbara
and an angel, who came and brought him the Holy Sac-
rament. This event caused the young man to renounce
the world and join the Jesuit Order in Rome, where he
died only a year later.

In 1583, a later tenant had the room where Kostka lived
turned into a little chapel. In 1742 it was rebuilt in its
present form. Unfortunately it is only open on the Saint's
Day, November 13. He is the patron saint of young people and was canonized in 1726.

By the way, the name of the street refers to the officials
who collected the wine taxes for the Bishop of Passau.
They inhabited this quarter. No. 8 is the quaint little restaurant "Das Ofenloch" (The Furnace Mouth, I suppose). It is called so, because right next to it there is a
passage leading through to what was once Ofenloch-
gasse (now Kleeblattgasse) and the furnace referred
to was that of the sword-makers who lived there. Take
a look at the old bakery at No. 10. Built in 1520, it
has been a baker's shop since 1542 and, true to the old
tradition, it still sells only goods baked on its own premises.

Judenplatz

Kurrentgasse opens directly on to Judenplatz. This was
the centre of the first Jewish quarter dating back to as
early as 1195. Here stood the synagogue, the cantor's

house, the Jewish hospital and it was this square which originally went by the name of Schulhof (see p. 108). At first, the Jews were made welcome in Vienna. They were under the direct protection of the reigning sovereign and played an important role in the finances of the Court. However, the fact that many members of the nobility, the Court itself, and also most of the patrician families in town, had borrowed money from the Jews which they were no longer able to repay, was probably the basic cause of the first pogrom in 1420. An anti-semitic wave swept Austria. The Jews were accused of poisoning wells, causing the plague, being in league with the Hussites and anything else that came to mind. Finally, a story spread that they had killed Christian children and had desecrated the Host. The reigning Duke Albrecht, under pressure himself, issued a decree that all Jews in Austria were to be arrested and their money and property confiscated. The luckier ones were merely banished; they were put in boats and sent floating down the Danube to Hungary, where King Sigismund granted them permission to stay. A great number–no less than 80 cartloads in Vienna alone–were sent to the stake and burnt. Some escaped this terrible fate by accepting baptism, others preferred to congregate in the temple with their rabbi. As there was no way out, they begged him to kill them, which he did, finally committing suicide himself.

Albrecht then gave orders to pull down the walls of the ghetto and gave the houses to Christians. It was not until the reign of Frederick III in 1463, that the Jews were allowed to return.

The first house on the right, No. 2, is the oldest house in the square, known as "Zum grossen Jordan" (Great Jordan). There is a relief on the wall, a reminder of the pogrom. It shows the baptism of Christ in the River Jordan and a Latin inscription is witness to the antagonistic feeling prevalent in Vienna at the time. Let me give you the full text in translation: "Through the River Jordan the bodies are cleansed from disease and evil; thus all hidden sinfulness takes flight. Therefore the flame rising furiously through the entire city in 1421 purged the horrible crimes of the Hebrew dogs. The world was once cleansed by the deucalionian floods but this time punishment came by means of raging fire."

On the site of house No. 3/4 there used to be one of the houses where Mozart lived, although his stay only lasted just over one year.

Across from it, No. 11, is the back of the Bohemian Court Chancellery–a Fischer von Erlach building whose front looks out on Wipplingerstrasse, but as that part was badly damaged, the side facing Judenplatz is today, probably the more spectacular one.

In the centre of the square stands a statue of Lessing, the German writer who was the first to make a plea for tolerance with regard to Jews in his famous play "Nathan the Wise".

Just one more word about the square as such. Towards the end of the 17th century it was much frequented by strolling players, tightrope walkers, fire-eaters and other similar entertainers.

In the right-hand corner of the square, Jordangasse opens and we shall follow its winding course till we get to Schultergasse. The famous architect Fischer von Erlach lived at No. 5. It is a very short lane, bringing us out on to Tuchlauben once more.

Tuchlauben (2)

Immediately opposite where we emerge from Schultergasse is No. 20 Tuchlauben. The building, as such, is typical of the turn of the century, but on its facade at the corner, in a niche on the first floor, it has inherited a small statue of a 16th century peasant in hood and cape, warming himself over a primitive brazier. This statue was for many centuries on the previous house, a popular beer tavern by the name of "Winterhaus". The two markets, the farmers' and the fishers', were close together, creating a certain rivalry. The fishermen had, by law, to sell their goods standing bareheaded and without a coat (to cut short all possible haggling). Very likely the little man—obviously a farmer—on the Winter Beer House was set up to make fun of the fish vendors. On the other hand the statue may well symbolize "Winter".

But let us turn right down Tuchlauben until we reach No. 19. From the outside it is an early 18th century building—not anything so unusual in Vienna. Therefore, it was a veritable sensation when murals dating back to the year 1400 were discovered inside it in 1979. They are the oldest secular paintings in Austria and illustrate poems by the minnesinger Neidhard von Reuenthal (see p. 11). The site is now a museum and certainly worth a visit, for it is not every day that one can see paintings more than 550 years old. Besides which the light-hearted scenes from medieval life are very enjoyable. The first shows a peasants' mock tournament, followed by a ball game which ends in a love-scene. Next, a girl is about to lose her "mirror", a euphemistic term for virginity in those days. There are also remnants of a pretty winter sleighride. But the best preserved part is the procession leaving Court, with music and dancing to hail the arrival of the first violet in the Vienna Woods (see p. 11).

The premises were once a large festive hall belonging to a certain wealthy cloth merchant by the name of Michael Menschein, or Mondschein.

As you have already seen the other end of Tuchlauben, we will retrace our steps, cross Schultergasse and shortly we arrive at the corner of Hoher Markt and Wipplingerstrasse. Before turning into the latter, let us cross the street and stand under the clock at the corner of Marc-Aurel-Strasse. As the street is of little interest otherwise, just pause here a moment to remember that it is named after a Roman Emperor who was in Vienna no less than three times and is supposed to have died in the Roman camp here in 180 A.D. It is even likely that this philosopher-soldier completed his "Meditations" in Vienna shortly before his death.

Having paid our tribute to Rome, we will proceed down Wipplingerstrasse.

Wipplingerstrasse

At one time it was known as "Wildwercherstrasse" as it was the skinners and furriers who plied their trade in this area.

When we enter the street coming from Hoher Markt, the first houses in no way prepare us for the ones following: to the left the magnificent Bohemian Chancellery. It suffered from the ravages of two wars, once in 1809 and again in 1945. Now the only part of the original Fischer von Erlach building still standing on Wipplingerstrasse is the eastern half of the facade. At this time it is the seat of the Administrative and Constitutional Court.

On the other side of the street, at No. 8, stands the old Town Hall. It first appears in the chronicles of the year 1435. The front was redesigned in the 18th century and the Council Chamber received its elaborately decorated ceiling at about that time.

The central courtyard encloses the lovely Andromeda Fountain by Georg Raphael Donner.

Since the City Council moved to the Neue Rathaus, this building has been used as offices for the district administration. In addition, the Museum of the Resistance Movement and the Museum of the First District are incorporated in this complex. The latter possesses pictures of various events mentioned in this book.

But the Rathaus was not only used for the administration of the city, it was also occasionally the scene of executions. We have a very detailed description of one of these:

In the 17th century there lived an extremely wealthy Hungarian Count, Nádasdy by name, who got himself involved in a conspiracy for Hungarian independence.

The Andromeda Fountain

The plot was discovered and all the conspirators sentenced to death. Nádasdy was to have his right hand chopped off first and then lose his head into the bargain, this being the usual penalty for traitors. Emperor Leopold I is said to have shown extreme clemency by altering this terrible sentence to mere beheading; the Count's hand was to be spared!

Nádasdy was brought from his prison to the Rathaus on April 27, 1671. After he had taken leave of his retinue, he was led away to the large subterranean hall. Priests and guards accompanied him. In the hall there was an altar, decked out with black cloth and a black chair stood on a black carpet. The Count sat on the chair and once again the sentence was read out to him, including the merciful pardon concerning his right hand. He then called his favourite page and had him unbutton his coat, tidy his hair and blindfold his eyes. This done, the Count folded his hands and began to call out loudly "Jesus and Mary". When he had repeated these words seven times, the executioner swung his sword and severed the head with a single blow.

Three masked men immediately stepped forward, took the bloody corpse, put it in a coffin, set the head with its open, staring eyes on its breast and carried it up into the courtyard of the town hall, where it was displayed to the public (roughly where the fountain is situated today). Thousands of citizens thronged to see the earthly remains of the traitorous Count. It was a big sensation. (See illustrations at the Museum of the First District.)

To the left of the Andromeda Fountain a passage leads out into Stoss im Himmel. On the way to this street, many reproductions from the City Museum are exhibited. They are interesting and one should take the time to look at them more closely.

Stoss im Himmel

A strange name this: a push into heaven. Originally it applied to a certain house in this street which is supposed to have belonged to a rich woman. She loved beautiful clothes more than anything else and her greatest pleasure was to walk down the street, with all the people staring after her in admiration. Her pride was such that she even made fun of a statue of the Virgin Mary by haughtily exclaiming: "How poor your clothes are as compared to mine. Can't you do better than that as Queen of Heaven?"

It was not long after this that a strange thing happened. There was a knock at the door at midnight and when the servants unwillingly opened it, they found an old beggar-woman outside who demanded to be led to the lady of the house. At first the maids tried to persuade her to come back in the morning so as not to disturb their mistress at such an hour, but the old woman was insistent and they finally led her upstairs.

The rich woman was angry at being awoken by a beggar. "I am not here to beg," replied the withered crone, "I have something in my basket which is worth all your riches and more. It is a dress fit for a queen. Do you want to see it?" At first the lady was sceptical. What kind of dress could a ragged old woman possess? But her curiosity got the better of her and she asked to see it. And true enough, the dress which the woman drew from the basket took her breath away. Never had she seen anything so costly, so unique. It was truly a royal garment made of the finest silks and satins, studded with precious stones and glittering with gold. "My good woman," she exclaimed, "I must have that dress. Tell me quickly how much it will cost." "You'll never be able to pay for it," replied the old hag, "because all your money is gone, your coffers are empty." "That's only too true," sighed the lady, "but I'll sell all my possessions if only I can have that one lovely, lovely gown."

"No matter what you sell, you'll never get enough to pay for this dress, my dear. But as you seem to have set your heart on it, I have a suggestion. I'll let you have the dress for three days and three nights. At midnight on the third night I'll come and fetch it and as my reward I shall get whatever happens to be covered by the dress at that time."

To this the rich woman agreed. It would at least give her three days in which she could parade the streets in her new splendour. She hardly heard what the old woman said, she was so eager to slip the gown on.

The dress was a perfect fit, it seemed expressly made for her. For a long, long time she stood admiring her reflection in the mirror and could not bring herself to take it off again. As soon as it got light she went out into the street. The vain woman was delighted that everyone turned to stare at her in amazement and all those who saw her in this beautiful garment were envious. What bliss it was to be the talk of the town, even if only for three days!

As the end of the third day drew near, the lady suddenly had misgivings, remembering what the old woman had said. She went home and tried to take off the dress, but to her horror, she found that it stuck to her body and no matter how she tugged and pulled, she could not get it off. The maids had all gone to bed and there was no one around to aid her. In her terror she realized that it had been the devil who had so tempted her and whose prey she had so easily become. "I'll tear it to pieces," it flashed across her mind. But the material would not give an inch. Just then the clock struck midnight and no sooner had the last sound died away than the door opened and the old beggar-woman entered. "Well, my dear, I must say that dress suits you very well," she cackled. "But I trust you remember our agreement: whatever is covered by the dress at midnight shall be mine. It covers you and therefore you are mine!"

There was a peal of thunder, the room was filled with a fiery glow and the old woman had turned into the devil. Moreover, the dress, too, had changed: the cloth of gold had become glowing embers which gave forth little yellow flames. In her terror and despair the lady fell to her knees and prayed fervently that her vanity be forgiven her, promising to repent her sins. As a last resort, she clasped a medal of the Virgin Mary which she wore around her neck, but the devil stretched out his claws towards her. At that instant she received a vigorous push, by an invisible hand, which thrust her out of the devil's reach. Immediately the burning dress crumbled and fell away from her body and Satan tore out of the window, roaring and cursing horribly.

This push was veritably a push into heaven, for the lady changed her life completely thereafter. She withdrew from the worldly life she had heretofore led and went into a convent where she remained until her death. But the house in which this event is supposed to have taken place was forthwith called "A push into heaven".

The street is actually named for one Josefa Cornelia Stosanhiml who lived at No. 3 during the time of King Ottokar.

We walk down to the right to Salvatorgasse. Looking left, we catch our first view of Maria am Gestade and it is to this church that we will go next.

Maria am Gestade

St. Mary's on the Riverside, also called St. Mary's at the Stairs, is said to have been built in 882. Presumably some small chapel did stand there at that time, but be that as it may, the church was already being enlarged by 1154.

It is interesting that while the Dukes of Austria were busy building the choir of St. Stephen's, it was the citizens of Vienna who took it upon themselves to build, enlarge and embellish St. Mary's on the Riverside, also paying the priests who read mass.

By 1414, the nave had been finished; it is narrower than the choir because there was no possibility of expansion. On the one side, there was the steep cliff down to the banks of the Danube, on the other, even at that time, were the houses of Salvatorgasse.

During the reforms under Joseph II, the church was to be demolished, luckily, however, it proved too expensive an undertaking, so it was left standing. Nevertheless, it was secularized and, in 1809, served the army as a stock-room.

By 1812 it was once again used as a church, this time for the Czech population which thronged to Vienna seeking work.

Coming from Stoss im Himmel, we get our first breathtaking glimpse of the glorious tower of St. Mary's. It is perhaps interesting to note that it is built on a septagonal base which is, no doubt, connected with the mysticism of numbers very prevalent in the Middle Ages (in this case referring to the seven gifts of the Holy Spirit, the seven sacraments and the seven virtues). The steeple is one of the most exquisite examples of Gothic tracery architecture.

As we approach, the first portal already tempts us to enter, but let us merely admire the Madonna of the Protective Mantle on the left and the Coronation of the Virgin Mary on the right above the door and then go on to the next entrance. On the way you will notice quite high on the wall between the two porches a tin roof which seems to serve no purpose. When the church was being renovated in the 1930's a huge painting of St. Christopher was uncovered here. The roof was intended to shield it from the weather. This it may have done successfully, however, the air pollution of later decades has effaced every trace of the painting.

The second door on Salvatorgasse has a relief of four little angels above it; one with a hand organ, another with an aspergill, a third with a lute and the fourth with a book. And it is here that we will enter.

One of the fascinating facts about this church is that it is built at an angle and if you stand in the nave just inside the door and look towards the altar, you will notice this phenomenon: The choir is not a straight prolongation of the nave, but at a slight angle to it because the northern outer wall was built on top of part of the ancient Roman Camp.

St. Mary's has its own special saint. It is the priest Klemens Maria Hofbauer, who is the patron saint of Vienna. He is buried and revered in the chapel under the tower on the right side of the nave. The wall next to the chapel is studded with plaques donated in gratitude for prayers answered by this saint. This chapel also holds the two panels of the original Gothic main altar, long since removed (dated approx. 1460).

Also on a column beside the chapel is a statue of the Virgin Mary and opposite it on a corresponding column on the other side of the nave, the angel of an annunciation group (approx. 1340).

Among the other marvels of this church are the three stained glass windows behind the main altar (approx. 1350–1436). It is only due to the fact that they were taken out and evacuated to Styria that we can admire them today, for in the last war this church, too, caught fire and most of the remaining windows were damaged.

In order to protect the stained glass and save it from the fate of the St. Christopher painting, an extra layer of glass has been added on the outside. We now walk right up to the altar. Near the communion rail there is a small doorway on the left with a notice "Zum Pergeraltar". Although the detour does not seem very promising at this point, do go on. Inside you will find yourself in a dark room. You may easily think you have made a mistake, but do not give up, turn into the small door to your left where you will find a light-switch. Here in a little chapel you will come face-to-face with one of the loveliest altars in Vienna. As the writing conveys, it was dedicated by one Johann Perger in 1520 and this cleric is portrayed kneeling on the left. In the middle there is the Virgin Mary with the Holy Child, flanked by St. John the Baptist with a lamb and St. Nicolas with the three golden balls. How this jewel came to be so tucked away that most people know nothing of its existence, I do not know.

Returning to the church, we now walk down the aisle on the right. The second chapel on the right has net vaulting and a tiny window at the very top (best seen from the further side of the nave). It encloses a medieval pane with the coat-of-arms of the Liechtenstein family, the lily; the Liechtensteins contributed considerably towards the construction of the church and had originally hoped it would be the site of their family tomb.

At the far end of the nave on the right, is the tombstone of yet another potential local saint, the priest Wilhelm Janauschek. He was very popular among his congregation and though he has not yet been canonized, he seems to have more followers nowadays than his predecessor Hofbauer.

At this point I would like to mention that lovely concerts are sometimes held in this church especially before Christmas. And it is indeed a treat to hear music in a setting such as this–and in an atmosphere laden with the devoutness of past generations.

Finally, let us leave by the porch through which we came in and go forward to the front of the church. The hanging stone canopy above the main entrance which, unfortunately, is always closed, is an amazing piece of architecture. Then bend as far back as you can and gaze up at the fantastic gargoyles jutting out on the sides of the roof.

Before we descend the steep steps, a short visit to Schwertgasse on the left is recommended.

Schwertgasse

It owes its name to house No. 3, "The Seven Swords". Built between 1710 and 1720, it has a large coat-of-arms featuring the seven swords above the door held by two little cherubs. The seven swords are those that pierced the heart of the Virgin Mary, which also explains the pietà over the lintel.

Inside this house, a door leads to the stairs on the left, at the bottom of which we come unexpectedly upon a beautiful Baroque statue of St. Rochus. As this is a saint little known in Anglo-Saxon countries, it might be the place to mention a few words about him. He was born around 1290 in Southern France and in 1317 made a pilgrimage to Rome. As the plague was at that time raging

The Sign of the Seven Swords, Schwertgasse

throughout Italy, he began to care for the sick. Finally, he too fell ill and no one bothered to nurse the stranger. He dragged himself to a hut in the woods, where a dog came and brought him a loaf of bread every day. After he recovered, he was accused of spying and thrown into prison, where he died five years later. He is often shown as a pilgrim, with a hat and staff, one knee exposed to reveal a sore. Beside him there is usually a dog with a loaf of bread in its mouth. Rochus is a popular saint in Austria and you will often find statues of him in churches.

Back to Passauerplatz in front of Maria am Gestade and this time we will go down the steps. Below there are three old and rather lovely houses: No. 1 was built in 1616, though the facade is presumably about 1800, but the other two are remnants of the 16th century.

One last farewell glance back at Maria am Gestade and then we turn left into Tiefer Graben.

Tiefer Graben

Having turned into Tiefer Graben, we look over at No. 23 on the right side of the road–the site of a well-known brothel in the Middle Ages.

The same site, however, has an amusing story connected with a house that stood there in the times of Emperor Joseph II. A civil servant had bought it and because he was such an admirer of the Emperor's, he called it "The Emperor Joseph" and used the Monarch's image as his house sign. When he was reprimanded and told this would not do, he felt it was a waste of a perfectly good house sign and simply had the portrait painted over, changing the sign's name to "St. Joseph". After a while, however, the paint began to peel off the lower part of the picture and finally there was St. Joseph, with a halo and a beard, wearing an Austrian general's uniform, decorated with a row of medals.

We are now about to go under the Hohe Brücke, the bridge which spans Tiefer Graben. There have been bridges at this point for hundreds of years and pictures of two of these are shown to the left and right on the bridge itself. On the other side of the bridge, No. 22 has a plaque on a level with the street above, proclaiming that a city gate stood here during Babenberg times.

On the left, we shortly reach another of Mozart's habitations, No. 18, where he resided in 1773. It has a pretty wrought-iron doorway which, unfortunately, is always locked.

Next door, at No. 16, is a lovely old house from the second half of the 18th century, with delightful pediments richly carved over the windows.

The new house, bearing Nos. 8–10, has a modern mosaic to remind us that Beethoven lived here from 1815–1817.

No. 6 is a really old house, the other end of which we shall encounter and discuss more fully when coming to Am Hof (see p. 125).

And this brings us to the corner of Heidenschuss. We shall not linger here, as this area is described elsewhere (Fifth Tour, p. 159), but turn left till we reach the large square Am Hof.

Am Hof

An ancient square indeed. It was here that the first town residence of the Babenberg Dukes was built, am Hof meaning "at Court". In 1165, Henry II (Jasomirgott) and his wife Theodora gave a feast for Frederick I (Barbarossa) which lasted two weeks. At this Court the famous minnesinger Walther von der Vogelweide wrote and sang. Later it was used as a market place, but sometimes also as a place of execution. It was here that Count Ferdinand of Hardegg was beheaded for having relinquished the fortress Raab to the Turks without dire necessity. Emperor Rudolph II sentenced him to death for this, as an example of what happened to traitors.

It was a macabre spectacle. A podium covered in black cloth was prepared. The Count bids his followers farewell, steps forward, gives a short speech protesting his innocence and asking the crowd to pray for him. He then bares his neck and right arm himself and kneels down on the velvet cushion prepared for him. He kisses the cross the priest holds out and lays his right hand on the block. The executioner comes forward, bows to him and one of his apprentices chops off the white aristocratic hand. Almost immediately the executioner swings the huge sword, which the Hardegg family has had especially made for this purpose and the head rolls down. The crowd gives a loud shout of admiration for the headsman's art. The Hardegg retinue now takes the headless body and it, together with the head and hand, are put in a magnificent coffin. This is loaded on to a hearse drawn by six horses and the funeral procession forms, moving off towards the Freyung.

This dramatic performance is followed by a grotesque and horrible comedy. The other culprit to be beheaded is the master builder of the fortress. He is a fat man with a very short neck. His hand is immediately severed, but the executioner has to strike twice at his neck–the blood flows in streams and the dying man roars like an ox being slaughtered. The people are so disgusted with this lack of skill that they start throwing stones at the executioner and it is only with the help of the city guards that he and his apprentices get away.

To take your mind off such gruesome stories there is a more pleasant memory which this square conjures up: it served as the site for the annual Christmas market from 1842–1929 and again from 1939–1945. In the weeks before Christmas, it was crowded with little booths, lit by oil lamps, selling decorations for the Christmas tree, candles and the like, as well as toys and candy. (This pretty scene can be admired at the District Museum, see p. 113).

Now let us look at some of the lovely houses. On the left is the Märkleinsche Haus which is now the garage of the Vienna Fire Brigade. In this house, the Viennese Mayor Liebenberg, who was in office during the second Turkish Siege, died only a few days before the relief armies arrived and liberated the city.

Right next to it is a very narrow red house, the 16th century house which we have already seen from the other side on Tiefer Graben.

The armour-clad angels Am Hof

In the left corner is the Bürgerliche Zeughaus (the Citizens' Armoury), which can be traced back to the 15th century. Citizens were actually supposed to supply their own arms, but it soon seemed advisable to have a public stock of arms so that all the members of a company would have more or less uniform equipment. The Turkish War of 1529 also proved the necessity for storing weapons and ammunition.

Underneath this Armoury are traces of the Roman Camp, which, at given times, are open to the public.

Walking the length of the square we reach No. 12, a pretty Baroque house in which the well-known Urbani Keller is located. Next to it is the Collalto Palais, where Mozart is supposed to have been a frequent guest.

The church is dedicated to the Nine Choirs of Angels. It is Gothic at the core, but this can only be seen from the back which juts out on to Steindlgasse (see p. 104). The facade and interior are Baroque. Originally built by the Carmelite monks, it later came into the possession of the Jesuits.

Before leaving Am Hof, just a few words about the lovely slender column with the 17th century statue of the

Virgin Mary which graces the square's centre. In 1818, it was described as follows: "The whole thing weighs 205 cwt., is of metal and not regarded very highly in the world of art"–how tastes do change! Round the base are four beasts: a snake, a dragon, a basilisk and a lion (symbolizing plague, war, famine and heresy). These monsters are being overthrown by armour-clad angels.

With our back to this column, let us now head towards the left-hand corner of the square where we find the shortest lane in town: Irisgasse.

Irisgasse

Short as it is, this lane has probably got the distinction of having been renamed more often than any other street in Vienna.

Today it goes by the name Irisgasse, there having been a shop at the corner in 1862 with the sign of an iris (or possibly the goddess Iris?). In the 17th century, however, it was called Hundsfottgässel (Dog's Fart Lane). It was here that a favourite Carnival pastime, the Adam-and-Eve Play, was performed every year. It must have been a rather boisterous affair, causing considerable disturbance, because Emperor Charles VI decreed in 1719 that it take place during the last three days of the Carnival season only and Maria Theresa forbade it altogether. Due to this connection, the street was also referred to as Adam-and-Eve Lane. But that still wasn't the end of its varying appellations. In the 19th century, it was known for a while as "Glockengasse" (Bell Lane) on account of a bell foundry situated there. At one time it went by the name of "Zweihäusergässel" (Two-House-Lane) which appropriately describes it. There is no doubt, however, that for so small a passageway it has had a lively history.

We walk the few steps down it and pause at the corner of Naglergasse.

Naglergasse

This area was at one time populated by the *needle*-makers–not by the nail-makers, as one might suppose.

It is a very old street and because it has retained its medieval narrowness it is rather difficult to appreciate the facades in all their glory.

At one time it was also a most fashionable street with several bathhouses. In those days (some 800 years ago), these were the substitute for our coffee-houses, bars and clubs.

Almost opposite Irisgasse, slightly to the right, No. 13 boasts a lovely relief of the Coronation of the Virgin above the door.

A sign at the corner of Naglergasse and Haarhof advertises the Esterházykeller. Twenty-seven very steep steps lead down into it. At the top of the staircase there is a notice claiming that "At the time when Vienna was besieged by the Turks in 1683, the defenders of the city gathered here in this cellar to drink Prince Esterházy's wine, a beaker of which was supplied free to each man".

The cellar is worth a visit and–unlike other wine-drinking places–it is open on weekdays from 10 a. m. to 1 p. m. In the beginning, this was a place for real drinkers, for no less than 1 liter of wine were served and it was not until 1828 that one could order a mere "Viertel". As for the name "Haarhof" (Hair Court), it refers to flax which was sold here.

No. 4 still bears the designation "Zum Bogner" (The Bowmaker) and leaves no doubt as to the vicinity of the Bowmaker's Street. At the end of Naglergasse a slab above the doorway of No. 2 commemorates the fact that the ancient Roman town wall stood here and remains of the Roman Camp were found when the present house was built in 1801.

At the corner of Graben/Naglergasse there was once a fortified tower, the "Peilertor", which led to Tuchlauben. Originally, it was a watchtower, later becoming a prison. In the 17th century there were shops downstairs, one of which belonged to a confectioner, Cecily Krapf. It seems that one day she happened to have a pan of boiling fat on the stove and accidentally dropped a piece of yeast dough into it. Within a few minutes it had turned into what proved to be a delicious dessert. At first these doughnut-like cookies were sold under the name Cilly (short for Cecily) Kugeln, but later, and to this day, they are known as Krapfen: a Viennese speciality during the Carnival season. The Krapf family became so wealthy and famous that one of the descendants bought a piece of property on the slopes of Kahlenberg which is still called Krapfenwaldl (it is now one of Vienna's best-known outdoor swimming pools).

If you wish to return to St. Stephen's just walk all the way to the end of Graben which is described in detail in the Fifth Tour (p. 161).

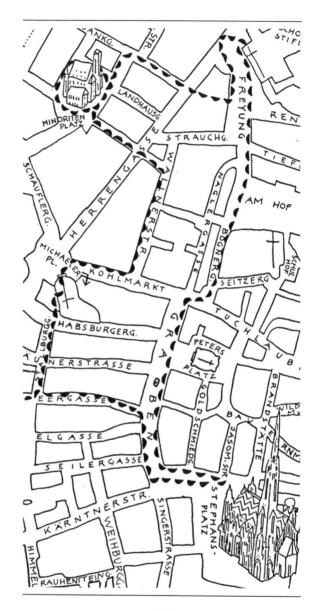

FIFTH TOUR

Stephansplatz
Stock-im-Eisen-Platz
Dorotheergasse
Stallburggasse
Michaelerkirche
Michaelerplatz
Kohlmarkt
Wallnerstrasse
Herrengasse
Minoritengasse
Bankgasse
Palais Ferstel
Freyung
Heidenschuss
Bognergasse
Graben

Stephansplatz

Once more unto the breach, dear friends–we will start again at the main entrance of St. Stephen's Cathedral. We are standing close to the stairway down to the subway station underneath the square. A quick detour underground will, think, prove rewarding.

While digging to install this subway beneath Stephansplatz, the workmen came across the foundations of the church of St. Magdalen's. This church was the seat of the Brotherhood of Notaries and Clerks. It was also used as a burial chapel and its crypt was a charnel house where the bones of those buried in the cemetery surrounding St. Stephen's were stored. But digging deeper, the workmen discovered the vaults of yet another chapel. True, 14th century chronicles mention a chapel "underneath the charnel house of St. Stephen's cemetery". This had always been confusing, but what turned out to be even more confusing now that this chapel had been discovered, was the fact that it was found to be at least a century older than art historians had presumed. According to recent estimations, this shrine must have been built at roughly the same time as the Giant Gate of St. Stephen's, but there is no mention of any such chapel. This in itself is strange. Stranger still is the fact that a well was found in front of the chancel. And strangest of all: there was no access–no trace of doors or stairs. The only means of entry could have been a trapdoor from above. This gave rise to a rumour that it might have been a hiding place, a place of refuge. But for whom? Or was it merely a building project that had to be abandoned due to lack of funds? It might, for instance, have been planned as an elaborate tomb for St. Coloman (see p. 18) but that nothing came of the project.

Now the chapel goes by the name of St. Virgil, because one of the altars mentioned in the 14th century crypt, when it was the burial vault of the Chrannest family, was dedicated to this saint. But still no one really knows why it was built and for whom.

There is a large window on the first level where the tick-

St. Virgil's Chapel

ets are sold; through this one can look into the renovated
St. Virgil's Chapel–a free service, no doubt unique in the
world today, offered to travellers along with their trans-
portation.
But let us return to ground level.

Stock-im-Eisen-Platz

At the corner of Kärntner Strasse and Graben there is a niche. This is where the famous Stock-im-Eisen (iron tree stump) stands. This "iron tree stump" is actually standing on its head. What seems like branches at the top are, in fact, the roots. It may be the sole survivor of a wood that once covered that area, a tree at the boundary of some sacred grove which, once the gods worshipped there had been dethroned, was uprooted and stuck in the ground upside down to signify the downfall of the ancient deities. In the chronicles, it is not mentioned until 1533, but is believed to be much older.

Every journeyman coming to Vienna had to hammer a nail into the stump to ensure a safe return home. It is not certain when this custom first came into practice, but the last nail was driven into it in 1832.

The Viennese are much attached to this ancient landmark and, to give some indication of their feelings, the following should perhaps be mentioned:

During the German occupation, there was talk of removing the Stock-im-Eisen and incorporating it into a locksmith museum in Frankfurt. Before this could be put into effect, suddenly one night the old tree had gone. It was not until the last flames of the terrible fire of the Cathedral had been successfully extinguished and the last German had withdrawn in the face of the on-coming Russian army, that the Stock-im-Eisen reappeared in its little niche again as suddenly as it had vanished.

The legend connected with this nail-studded tree tells of a locksmith's apprentice who made a pact with the devil. Satan demanded the boy's soul in return for making him rich and famous, but made the bargain seem more palatable by assuring him it was only valid if the boy ever missed a Sunday mass. The apprentice thought this a fair risk and agreed.

Shortly after the devil appeared at the smithy, in disguise of course, and ordered an iron band for the tree near St. Stephen's. It was to have an intricate lock which only one key could open. No one dared to try his hand at it,

Court of the Equitable Palais

until the young apprentice spoke up and asked to be allowed to accept this order. His efforts were crowned
with success, the band was put around in the tree, the
lock put in place and the devil left with the only key.
As was customary the boy, now a journeyman, went
abroad and did not return to Vienna until many years la-

ter. Here he found that the City Counsellors were offering a reward to anyone who could open the lock on the "Stock-im-Eisen". The young locksmith immediately went to work and despite the devil's interference, was able to forge the key and open the lock. It was a masterpiece and he became famous and rich. Moreover, he thought he had outwitted the devil by always attending mass on Sunday.

But Satan found ways to get his due. He saw to it that the wealthy locksmith fell in with bad company and one Sunday the inevitable happened. Too involved in gambling and drinking the locksmith suddenly heard the bells of St. Stephen's chiming out noon. He rushed to the Cathedral, but it was too late. When he reached the main gate, he was only in time to hear the priest's "Ite, missa est" (Go, the mass is ended). Immediately there was a thunderous noise of wings beating the air and a huge, ugly demon swooped down to disappear with the hapless man.

Nos. 3–4, next to the tree, the Equitable Palais, was named after the "Equitable Life Insurance Company of New York". On its door panels are reliefs of the Stock-im-Eisen legend. During office hours this building is open and though from the outside it is not very prepossessing, you should–if the opportunity arises–go inside. It is one of the best examples of Historicism and the staircase, hallway and glass-covered court are quite extraordinary.

We are now going further down Graben, but will revert to its history and points of interest on our way back. For the time being, let us walk as far as Dorotheergasse and turn into it.

Dorotheergasse

An old street this, the name being connected with the monastery and church that once stood here. It was an elegant area, for apart from this monastery, and another convent across from it, by the 17th century practically every house belonged to some member of the aristocracy. Though some of these palaces have since disappeared, there are still several beautiful mansions along this street.

Shortly after turning into it, we pass No. 3, the Graben Hotel, where, as a plaque reminds us, such literary celebrities as Franz Kafka and his biographer, Max Brod, were frequent guests. Peter Altenberg, a Viennese writer of the Schnitzler/Hofmannsthal generation and a legend even in his lifetime, even became a permanent resident.

On the opposite side of the street, at No. 6, there is a coffee-house, the Hawelka, a meeting place for both genuine and would-be artists and their retinue. A little further on we come upon the famous music shop, Doblinger, a veritable treasure trove for any music lover.

On the left, No. 9, is the Starhemberg Palais, built at the beginning of the 18th century. The first of that line to be named as owner of the site is the famous Ernst Rüdiger von Starhemberg, the valiant commander and defender of Vienna during the Turkish Siege of 1683. The palace, however, was only built after he died.

Further up the street, at No. 17, is the Dorotheum. It is the official City Auction and Pawnbroker's Institution, lovingly called "Aunt Dorothy" by the Viennese. The fact that is was once the site of the ancient monastery of St. Dorothy is still evident in the courtyard to the left of the main entrance–unfortunately only open during the week. Someone has rescued a few, badly damaged remnants of tombstones found when the old church and monastery were demolished and set them in the wall. Across on the other side, we see the Protestant church at the corner. Around 1581, Queen Elisabeth, daughter of Emperor Maximilian II and widow of the French King Charles IX, founded a convent here and retired to it.

Her life had been a tragic one; she was betrothed to Charles at the age of sixteen, had been in Paris during the horrors of St. Bartholomew's massacre and soon afterwards she lost both her husband and her only child, a daughter. A widow at twenty, she returned home to Vienna. Only two years later her father died, too. Her brother Rudolph II took his court to Prague and so Elisabeth decided to retire to a convent. Owing to her own presence there, as well as to the fact that both the church and the convent were dedicated to Mary, Queen of Angels, the nunnery was generally referred to as the Königinkloster (Queen's Convent).

It was the first to be abolished under Emperor Joseph II in 1782. This same Emperor, though, had also issued letters patent allowing free worship for all religions; the Lutherans were the first to take advantage of this freedom. They bought part of the premises of the erstwhile convent (now No. 18) and after making radical changes, they began using the building in 1783. However, in accordance with the stipulations the entrance to the church had to be at the back and they were not allowed to have a church tower.

Take a brief look at the pretty courtyard of No. 16 next door, with its yellow walls, overgrown with creeper. On the right, between the two semi-circular windows, you can see a plaque commemorating Joseph II. For the other denomination to profit by this liberal Monarch's decrees, was that of the Evangelical and Reformed (Presbyterian) Protestants, who built their church here at the corner of Dorotheergasse and Stallburggasse. And it is into this latter street that we now turn.

Stallburggasse

As soon as you turn the corner you are confronted with
a very pretty view: an incredible jumble of roofs at different levels, from the low one-storey house at the end of
the street (actually on Habsburgergasse) to the Romanesque walls of the transept, the Gothic roof and the slim
tower of St. Michael's.

We head directly towards the wide gate of the little
house in the foreground. The last block on your left is
the back of the stables where the White Horses of the
Spanish Riding School have their home (see p. 175). In
front of this building there is a very small shack. It is
Vienna's smallest antique store. Yes, this part of the city
is certainly a collector's paradise; practically every other
shop is either an art gallery or an antique store.

We cross Habsburgergasse and enter the gate underneath the lantern at No. 14. Through the much-weath-
ered doorway, with its pretty wrought-iron grill at the
top, we keep going and shortly the passage widens into a
court with shops on either side. At the other end, to your
right, a beautiful relief of "Christ on the Mount of
Olives" goes back to the year 1480; it is surprisingly well
preserved.

Immediately after it, under the archway, we come upon
the side entrance to St. Michael's and this is where we
enter the church.

Michaelerkirche

Inside the door, on your left, a suffering Christ looks
down at you: truly "a man of sorrows and acquainted
with grief"! Further on, we pass a pretty Baroque chapel
on the left and enter the church proper through the
glass-paned doors. Again, another chapel to the left and
here it might be of interest that–usually half-hidden by a

picture of the Virgin Mary to the fore–you can just catch a glimpse of the head of a man praying. This is a memorial to Austria's Chancellor, Engelbert Dollfuss, who was assassinated (see p. 190). And now to the church itself.

Like St. Augustine's (see p. 171), St. Michael's was used by the Court and dates back to the early 13th century, though many changes were made later. Because it was right outside the palace, the church's cemetery was a favourite burial site for members of the Court and today practically the entire floor of the church consists of old tombstones, which were moved inside when the cemetery was no longer used.

The partition between the entrance hall and the nave is closed during the lunch hour (12–3 p.m.).

Let us go first to the Chapel of St. Nicolas on the right side at the front; it has an interesting history. One Stibor Chrezzel, cook at the Court of Albrecht the Wise, had been accused of having tried to poison his master. When Albrecht was taken ill after a meal, the doctors had him hung by his feet and left him suspended for many hours. Though this drastic therapy certainly saved his life, he was ever after a cripple and went down in history as "Albrecht the Lame". But to get back to the unfortunate Chrezzel. He was to be executed, but at the very last minute he managed to prove that he was innocent. His accuser was put into the Fool's Cage on Hoher Markt, to be ridiculed by the mob (see p. 65); two weeks later he was immured at St. Stephen's. Chrezzel, however, had this chapel built in thanksgiving for his narrow escape. It was also to serve as a burial vault for him and his family.

One of the oldest tombstones can be seen to the left of the altar and commemorates Pankras von Plankenstein who died in 1465. The chapel was also the headquarters of the St. Niklas Guild, the Brotherhood of Musicians.

Although there are innumerable, sometimes very sumptuous tombstones in this church, I only want to point out one other to you. It is quite small and situated right beneath the pulpit. It shows a little girl in a gown with a ruff and reads tragically: "Anna Margareta Papazonin died this 16th July aged 8 months and 14 days 1619".

A fascinating, if somewhat gruesome, experience is a visit to the crypt of this church, if you can time it to coincide with one of the conducted tours (see annex). Many members of the nobility and courtiers are buried here and, due to the amazing consistency of the temperature, a kind of mummification has taken place. Some of the bodies, as well as the clothes in which they were buried, are well preserved. Thus one can see a lady in a silken gown, a courtier in knee-breeches and a short cloak, as well as a young woman who died in childbirth.

Before leaving the church, look up at one of the most lovely Baroque organs in town; it is now being restored. Perhaps I should also mention that there are sometimes tours of the adjoining monastery (located at Habsburger-gasse No. 11). These usually take place in June or September, but you would have to check with the Pfarramt for the exact dates. It is a tour of unexpected vistas and treasures, as for instance, an entire room full of ancient embroidered vestments.

Now let us go out through the main entrance into Michaelerplatz.

Michaelerplatz

Coming out of the church you are practically over-whelmed by the enormous complex on your left. This was one of the late additions to the Hofburg, though the blueprints are the work of Fischer von Erlach, and in 1889–1893 Ferdinand Kirschner used them. With the three patinated cupolas and the elaborate ironwork over the gate, the result is amazingly pleasing. Even the rather too copious statuary on the roofs, the burly Herculean men on both sides of the entrance and the dramatic fountains at the corners, representing supremacy at sea and on land, do not seem out of context. The entire wing is a tribute to the imperial power of the 19th century.

Originally, of course, the area around the church was a cemetery and only after burial within the city limits was forbidden, did it become a square.

Old prints show a strange annex jutting out from the wall of the palace to the left, about half-way between the central doorway and the fountain. This is where the old Burgtheater (Court Theatre) stood and there is still a plaque to commemorate this fact.

The house to the right, at the corner of Kohlmarkt, is called the Grosse Michaelerhaus. But as the entrance is on Kohlmarkt we shall revert to it when we get there.

Across from it, on the corner between Kohlmarkt and Herrengasse, stands a house of an entirely different epoch. It is the Looshaus, built by the architect Adolf Loos in 1911. It caused much angry debate and was disdainfully referred to as "the house without eyebrows" because it was the first building to dispense with the century-old custom of decorating windows with fancy pediments.

Before this house appeared on the scene, however, one famous for other reasons stood here. It was called the Dreilauferhaus (the House of the Three Runners). There is a story connected with it which I would like to tell you. In the 15th century an armourer by the name of Eschelbach lived here with his wife Margaret. He also employed a very handsome apprentice, Grünspömlein by name, and Mistress Margaret did not seem impervious to the looks this young man gave her. Before long, she was urging him to get rid of her husband. Together they started putting a powder in Eschelbach's food which was to kill him slowly. Indeed, the powder did its work: Eschelbach did not die suddenly, but became ill and before long went mad. When they threatened to put him in chains–the usual treatment for madmen in those days–he started raving and jumped out of the window. He died instantly from his fall, leaving the impression that he had committed suicide in a fit of insanity. Margaret married her lover and neither of them were suspected of having had a hand in a crime. Grünspömlein is supposed to have become a high-ranking politician and it was whispered

abroad that he used the method of the powder many a time to rid himself of unwanted competition, but for lack of evidence he could never be brought to justice.
We now make our way towards Kohlmarkt.

Kohlmarkt

Just a few words about the street as such. It was not, as some people erroneously presume, a cabbage market, but a market for wood and charcoal from very early times.
When entering Kohlmarkt the first house to your left is No. 11 (Grosses Michaelerhaus, see p. 142) and it has a courtyard you simply must not miss. You enter through a dark vestibule which, however, has a surprisingly beautiful stuccoed ceiling. Out at the other end and you find yourself in what today is a court where the garbage bins are kept. But that is by no means all this court has to offer. There are so many centuries united here: the Romanesque walls and roof, the Renaissance spire, as well as the small Baroque cupola of one of the side chapels of St. Michael's, the Baroque carriage houses, which are as pretty a sight as you are liable to find in Vienna, and across from them, the Pawlatschen-house with its open galleries. By the way, you can still see some of the windlasses on these balcony railings, with which heavy loads were hoisted upstairs to avoid lugging them up the many flights of steps.
It is in this house that Joseph Haydn lived in 1749. When his voice broke he could no longer remain a choir boy and was sent away. The verger of St. Michael's took him in, recommending him to a man living in the Grosse Michaelerhaus. Haydn was given a wretched little attic, which was particularly uncomfortable in winter as there was no stove. He kept himself alive by giving piano and singing lessons. There is no trace of this attic today, because a further floor was added to the house in 1848.

Baroque carriage houses, Kohlmarkt

Emerging from this little detour we get a good view of the entrance of the Manz Publishing Company which was designed by Adolf Loos, the architect who also built the house on Michaelerplatz (see p. 142).

Right next to it is the world-famous cake shop, Demel: "Imperial and Royal Confectioners", as it still proudly calls itself. The shop dates back to the year 1786. In that year a certain confectioner's apprentice by the name of Ludwig Dehne came to Vienna from Württemberg. He decided that an ideal place for a confectioner's shop would be opposite the old Court Theatre on Michaelerplatz (see p. 142) and he proved to be right. Unfortunately he died at the early age of twenty-nine, leaving his shop in the hands of his widow. This woman married her deceased husband's apprentice and the shop continued to thrive, later passing on to her son August. This young man was a veritable genius and achieved renown, not only as a confectioner, but also as a politican and soldier (during the revolution of 1848). However, *his* son was not interested in the business and the famous cake shop was sold to the head apprentice, Christoph Demel. When the old Burgtheater was torn down in 1888, Demel's moved to its present site on Kohlmarkt No. 14.

Opposite, at No. 9, there is a reminder that Frédéric Chopin stayed here from November 1829 to July 1830. But that was before the present Art Nouveau house was built by Max Fabiani in 1901.

This street is rather exciting in the diversity it offers. No. 10 on the other side is the Retti candle shop, the first of Hans Hollein's portals in Vienna (1965). At No. 7 on the other side of the road is his controversial, but very ornate jeweler's shop.

Before we turn into Wallnerstrasse to our left, it is worthwhile looking at the exquisite creations of the furniture shop at the corner. Thonet's bentwood chairs have lost nothing of their classic beauty and after almost 150 years are more popular than ever.

On this same site there used to be Milani's renowned coffee-house, founded in 1770. It was one of the first to offer its guests a great variety of local and foreign newspapers, which was to become a traditional characteristic of the genuine Viennese coffee-house.

The other corner, Kohlmarkt Nos. 8–10, was at one time a very well-known delicatessen store called "The Green Barrel". It belonged to a man called Spöttl, whose wife was a famous beauty. This lady was generally referred to as the "Anchovy Queen". She had many love affairs, among them one with the great statesman Metternich. She seems to have been particularly fond of this family because her affections were equally divided between father and son. The unavoidable confrontation gave the German playwright Kotzebue the idea for his comedy "The Two Klingsbergs" (1801).

Wallnerstrasse

Let us go down Wallnerstrasse. It is uncertain where the name originated. One version says that it comes from an old word for strange, referring to the many strangers who lived on this street; another claims that it may have been the cloth fullers who where responsible for the name (Tuchwalker).

Whatever the reason, it is an old street. On the site that is presently occupied by the Palais Esterházy, there is supposed to have been a hunting lodge belonging to the Babenberg Duke Leopold III (died 1136). The palace was built by Paul Esterházy in 1695. If you are lucky enough to find it open, do enter. To your right is a sign "Fürstenstiege" (Princes' Staircase), which is worth a glance, as is the courtyard straight ahead. It is one of those pleasant, creeper-covered retreats. Look up and you will see the tower with its old clock as well as the high chimneys on the roof.

The other place of interest is No. 8 further up the street, but it will suffice if we admire the statues of the portal from the corner of Fahnengasse. This is the Palais Geymüller and once housed the French Embassy. During the years of the French Revolution, Count Bernadotte was ambassador. On April 13, 1798, he had the new flag of the Republic, the Tricolore, hoisted. This act so infuriated the Viennese–one must remember that Marie Antoinette, one of Maria Theresa's daughters, had been beheaded by the Revolutionaries–that they tried to break open the door, smashed the windows and climbed up the statues to tear the flag down. They did, in fact, succeed and triumphantly bore the flag to the square Am Hof, where they burnt it, singing patriotic songs.

It is in commemoration of this event that the street to the left is called Fahnengasse (Flag Street). We will follow it until we reach Herrengasse.

Herrengasse

As the name implies, it was once the seat of the aristocracy due to its proximity to the Hofburg. There is no doubt that it is one of the oldest streets in the city and can be traced back to Roman times. Originally the main highway (Hochstrasse), it lay outside of the town limits and was not incorporated into Vienna proper until about 1270. When the Habsburg dynasty first moved into the Hofburg, this street became the centre for the aristocracy–practically every house was the town palace of some member of the nobility. By the beginning of the 16th century, when the Provincial Diet of Lower Austria built its "Landhaus" here, the name was changed to Herrengasse.

The house on the left corner of Fahnengasse und Herrengasse (Nos. 6–8) is Vienna's first American-style skyscraper, with its eleven floors (1933). Prior to its construction, the Liechtenstein family had their palace here from the 15th century onwards. It is here that the legendary Berta von Liechtenstein died. Upon the death of her husband, after a most unhappy marriage, she always wore widow's weeds of pure white. As this was not customary in Austria, it was held against her and was the only sin this pious woman was thought to have committed. At any rate, people believed this to be the cause of her finding no rest after her death and haunting the premises. This "White Lady" is said to appear shortly before some important event, be it good or bad, befalls the Liechtenstein family.

On reaching Herrengasse, the first house across the road is the Lower Austrian Museum. The building has two courtyards which are well worth seeing because they hold several very lovely exhibits, among them the old wrought-iron fountain (1570), which used to stand in the courtyard of the Landhaus next door.

This house (No. 13) is the seat of the Lower Austrian Diet. Unfortunately, the Landhaus is not open to the public, but from time to time there are tours and the janitor is very willing to tell you when these take place. But

Fountain in the Lower Austrian Museum, Herrengasse

even if you are unable to see the inside of this building, the two courts are worth visiting. At the far end of the second one, are two riders with the date 1571. One of them carries the ancient Austrian coat-of-arms (the bar), the other Rudolph's five eagles. To the left and right of the riders are hands wielding swords over a quaint notice, also dated 1571, which shows that the members of the Diet seem to have been a hot-headed crowd, for it admonishes them to refrain from carrying weapons when entering the premises and, under no circumstances are they to start brawling. Things must have been rather wild at the sessions in those days!

Leaving Herrengasse we proceed down Landhausgasse until we reach Minoritenplatz.

Minoritenplatz

This is indeed a palatial square, for there facing us is No. 4 with its gleaming, golden coat-of-arms, adorning the side entrance of the Liechtenstein Palais. No. 5, to the right, is the Palais Starhemberg, now housing two ministries, while No. 3 is the Palais Dietrichstein.

It is, however, the church that has given the square its name. The "fratres minores" (an order of mendicant friars) were sent to Vienna by St. Francis of Assisi at the request of Leopold VI. Several chapels preceded the present church, which was built in the late 14th century and today serves the Italian community in Vienna.

It was to this church that the victorious Rudolph von Habsburg had the body of his rival, King Ottokar of Bohemia, brought from the battlefield. As his corpse was carried naked into town, Rudolph's wife, Queen Anna, in pity, covered it with a purple cloth. After embalmment, Ottokar was laid out in the church for thirty weeks, then finally taken home to Bohemia.

Inside the church on the left wall is a large mosaic copy of Leonardo da Vinci's "Last Supper". Strangely it was Napoleon who was responsible for the creation of this copy. During his occupation of Milan, he wanted to have the entire wall of the convent, on which da Vinci's original is painted, taken down and moved to Paris. When this proved impossible, he had a copy made on canvas by the painter Bossi. Shortly afterwards, in 1806, he ordered a mosaic of the same masterpiece to be made by Giacomo Raffaelli. It took no less than eight years to complete. By that time, however, Napoleon was no longer in

The Church of the Minorite Friars

power and it was finally Austria's Emperor Francis I who bought it and had it brought to Vienna. It was not installed in its present position until 1847.

The inside of the church has changed considerably in the

course of the years, but part of the tympanon over the main entrance dates back to about 1350 and as we start our round of the building we come across some very old tombstones under the arches to the left. Above them there are also several lovely windows, Gothic in origin.

Having made our way to the back of the church, we can now see the tower which has a rather unusual shape. The top of the first tower was shot away in 1529, during the first Turkish Siege and replaced by the provisional roof it still bears today. Where the tower changes to an octagon, the master builder has left us a portrait of himself, which however, is barely discernible from below.

We must now return to the front of the church and then take Petrarcagasse which leads into Bankgasse.

Bankgasse

This street owes its name to the Austro-Hungarian National Bank which at one time stood at its end on Herrengasse–a prosaic explanation, whereas the street, in fact, has many an interesting tale to tell.

Where No. 1 now stands, there used to be four small, old houses, one of which had a most sinister name–the House of the Five Murders.

In the year 1500 a baker, a certain Leonhard Reisner, lived in this house. He had an apprentice by the name of Bartholomew, who, however, left his master before his term of service was up. On the night of November 23, this man returned, slipped into the house, crept up the stairs and killed his successor and the serving girl with a huge axe. The sleepy baker must have heard something, for he came out of his bedroom to see what was amiss. No sooner had he reached the landing than the axe felled him, too. The erstwhile apprentice then went into the master's bedroom and dealt the baker's wife a death-blow while she was fast asleep.

When he came downstairs, he found the baker's little seven-year-old daughter crouching fearfully at the bottom. She looked up at him with a sweet smile and said: "Dear Barthel, please don't hurt me, I'll give you my doll and show you where my father's keys are." But Bartholomew refused to listen and cut her throat.

Though he managed to flee to his home town of Regensburg, he aroused suspicion by living a gay life with the money he had stolen from the baker. Before long, he was arrested and, admitting to his heinous crimes, he was taken to Vienna by ship. Here he was sentenced to a most dreadful punishment–his fingers were to be cut off, one by one, then he was be pinched with hot irons, whereupon he was to be tied to a horse and dragged to all the five market squares of Vienna. Finally, he was to be taken out of town to the place of execution, where the executioner was to drive a stake into his entrails.

All this was done and when Bartholomew faced his executioner, he confessed his crimes. He told the watching crowd that all the other four murders did not weigh too heavily on his conscience, but he simply could not forget the smile on that sweet and gentle little girl's face. No punishment, he admitted, was too severe to atone for that crime.

Death by impaling had long been abolished, but for this particular culprit it was reactivated. The executioner, however, had had no practice in this art and when he drove the stake into the man's entrails, the poor criminal screamed: "You've got it in wrong, pull it out and try again . . ."

No. 2 across the street is the Palais Batthyány. This was the home of "Beautiful Lori", the only woman in whom Prince Eugene ever showed any interest. The Countess was the widow of Field Marshal Batthyány. Prince Eugene fell for her when already a very old man; he went to visit her almost every evening for a game of whist. When leaving her around ten o'clock, he would get into his carriage and immediately fall asleep. His old coachman, also very drowsy, would soon drop off, while his ancient valet, standing behind the box of the carriage, was peacefully dozing, too. When they saw the carriage coming, the Viennese would walk on tip-toe, whispering with hushed awe: "There must be almost three centuries asleep in that carriage."

Part of the palace had been turned into a hotel by the middle of the 19th century. The Hotel Klomser achieved a rather questionable fame in connection with a famous spy, for it was in this house that Colonel Redl committed suicide. Redl was a General Staff Officer and member of the Army Intelligence Service, and as such was in a position to handle even highly confidential documents. The Russian secret service had found out that Redl was a homosexual and in love with a young army officer. This enabled them to bribe him. The fact that Russia, Italy, Serbia and even France had been in possession of the deployment plans of the Austro-Hungarian Army long before the war began, no doubt influenced the First World War considerably.

The last act of this tragedy took place at the Hotel Klomser. On the afternoon of May 23, 1913 Redl asked his young friend to visit him at the hotel. There had been friction between them for some time and that afternoon there must have been a serious quarrel. When they parted, Redl must have been either very confused or he knew only too well what he was doing. Otherwise, it seems incredible that a spy who had been busy passing information to the enemy (or potential enemy) for so many years without arousing even a trace of suspicion, should now walk right into the trap set for him.

Down at the Main Post Office, a letter addressed to a certain Nikon Nizetas had been awaiting collection for months. As no one came to claim it and for want of a return address, the letter was opened. Surprisingly, it contained no less than 6,000 Crowns (today approximately AS 223,000). Thereupon, the secret service became interested in the matter and installed three of their agents in the building next to the Post Office, to be on hand should the mysterious Mr. Nizetas ever come to collect his letter. The girl behind the counter had been instructed. A special bell had been installed and should someone come to claim that letter she was to ring and summon the three waiting detectives. So when Redl went to the Post Office to collect this letter the ball was set rolling. A wild chase followed and–as in any good detective story–the spy finally gave himself away through carelessness. That same evening three officers appeared at the Hotel Klomser. They confronted Redl and accused him of high treason. When he did not deny it, they handed him a revolver and left. He was to take his own life.

For hours the three officers waited below on Herrengasse, listening for the shot. When, at five in the morning, they were still uncertain, one of them went up to Redl's room, the door was open and he went in. The colonel was lying dead on the floor, the revolver beside him. The suicide of an army officer, as such, would not have aroused too much comment–it was a frequent result of gambling debts or love-affairs–and the secret service, embarrassed to admit that one of their own ranks had committed high treason, had hoped to hush up the matter by simulating suicide. However, through the indiscretion of a locksmith, who had been summoned to break open Redl's desk and cupboards, the press got hold of the story and promtly let the cat out of the bag. Thus the "Redl Affair" became the most sensational scandal of the Austro-Hungarian Monarchy of the century.

We now cross Herrengasse and enter the Café Central.

Palais Ferstel

Before we enter the beautifully restored shopping mall, I suggest that you have a quick cup of coffee at the Café Central. Its elaborate doorway leads into the "hallowed halls" of the erstwhile famous literary café, where so many of Austria's most renowned writers gathered at the turn of the century.

Café Central

It is still an awesome moment on entering, to remember all the celebrities who spent so much of their time in the arcaded, roofed-in courtyard, with a staircase leading to the balcony overlooking the many small marble-topped tables. For not only writers, such as Franz Werfel, Alfred Polgar, Egon Friedell and Peter Altenberg, but also the architect Adolf Loos, the painter Albert Paris Gütersloh, Sigmund Freud and even Lenin and Trotzky (then known as Bronstein), made it their "home-away-from-home". Stefan Zweig has described the typical Vienna coffee-house atmosphere as follows: "It is actually a kind of democratic club, accessible to everyone for the price of a cheap cup of coffee, where each guest can sit for hours, talking, writing, playing cards, receiving mail and, above all, reading innumerable newspapers and magazines".

Let us leave the coffee-house by the exit at the left of the stairs; this brings us out into the centre of the mall beside the pretty "Donaunixen" (Danube nixie) fountain. Window-shopping the entire length of the arcade is a delight, but please do take time to admire the elaborate decoration on the walls, the arches, the ceiling and ironwork.

The young architect Heinrich Ferstel designed this multi-purpose building containing a bank, stock exchange, shopping mall and offices, as well as the coffee-house.

At the end of the passage we come out on to a square where we turn left.

Freyung

This designation for the square is of later date, for at first it went by the name "next to the Scots", a misnomer because the monks summoned by Heinrich Jasomirgott, who built them a monastery here in 1158, were actually Irish. These monks were given the privilege of granting sanctuary–which is what Freyung means.

We proceed along the left side of the square and at No. 3 come to the Palais Harrach. This family has been the owner of what was once a group of houses since 1623. By the end of the 17th century, the Harrachs linked these houses and it is even likely that the famous architect Lukas von Hildebrandt had a hand in the construction of their new residence. It is a pity that extensive alterations were made in 1845, and the bomb damage of 1944, did its part in destroying most of the outer charm

Austria Fountain, Freyung

of what once must have been a lovely building. Inside it is still very beautiful, but at the time of writing it is not open to the public.

To your right, in the centre of the square, is a column with a statue at the top. This is the Austria Fountain, with its allegorical figures of the Rivers Danube, Vistula, Po and Elbe. The lady with crown, lance and shield is Austria. There is an amusing story connected with this monument. Its sculptor, Ludwig Schwanthaler, had had the statues cast in Munich, he had then filled them full of cigars, intending to smuggle them across the border into Austria. Unfortunately, though, he fell ill upon arrival in Vienna and by the time he recovered, the fountain had been set up and there was no way of getting at the cigars!

We continue on the left, and cross the street to Nr. 4, the Palais Kinsky. This time there is no doubt that it is a Lukas von Hildebrandt palace (1713–1716); unfortunately only the two courtyards can be viewed. Shops have been installed in the erstwhile stables and carriage houses, there is even a hairdresser's incorporating the original horse boxes. The names "Whyte Melville", "Captain", "Pretty Polly" conjure up shades of their previous occupants. The palace has a magnificent staircase and festive hall on the second floor, but the occasions are extremely rare when one can get to see these.

Once more out on the square, the church dominates our view. The present one dates from the mid-17th century, but inside–to the left of the main altar–is Vienna's oldest statue of the Virgin Mary, supposedly the work of a lay brother. It is said to work miracles since that day in March 1645, when the entire Court came in procession to pray for deliverance from the Swedes, who where outside the city walls. It is a historical fact that the Swedish forces, although their strength sufficed to take the city, suddenly withdrew for no obvious reason.

We leave the church and this time start walking down on the other side of the square. House No. 7 near the church, once the priory built in 1774, was jokingly referred to as "the chest-of-drawers house".

The Viennese obviously thought it singularly ugly, this first bourgeois house with its simple utilitarian front. As it happens, it became a much copied style in the years to come.

The house at the corner of Renngasse, now a bank, was once a tavern called "The Golden Ostrich". It was here that the Shoemakers' Revolt broke out in 1721. The apprentices attacked the workshops, beat their masters and pillaged. The night watchmen started shooting, but the City guards merely looked on, because they sympathized with the apprentices. However, the revolt was quelled and the two ringleaders publicly hanged. Nevertheless, at least some of the shoemaker boys' demands were met (see p. 44).

At the other end of this building, another renowned tavern once stood "The Little Red Man". In the first half of the 16th century it was much frequented by artists and itinerant scholars. The legend goes that Dr. Faustus, while in Vienna, spent much of his time there. Once one of his artist friends, slightly the worse for drink, drew a picture of the devil on the wall. Faustus brought it to life by using magic and everyone was horrified to see Satan himself grinning down at them.

Heidenschuss

From the corner at the traffic lights you have a good view of the statue of a Turk with a scimitar on the corner house opposite and, though he bears no weapon to shoot with, he represents the "heretic shooting". The story connected with this name claims that during the first Turkish Siege of Vienna in 1529, the enemy had dug their mine trenches right under the city and were about to blow it up. A baker's boy, who happened to be in the cellar of the house at the bottom of Freyung, heard strange rumblings and rushed to raise the alarm, thus averting a catastrophe. In gratefulness for the boy's discovery, King Ferdinand rewarded the entire Bakers' Guild by letting it hold a solemn procession, with banners and music, every Easter Monday. The statue, however, must be of a later date for in the chronicles it is described as "a Turk with bow and arrow about to shoot", which does not apply to the present one.

The fact that the name of the house, "The Shooting Heretic" (Heidenschuss), is fully a century older–mention of it appearing in 1429–together with this description of a shooting Saracen connected with the house, has led historians to believe that it might have been named after the Viennese Mayor Haiden, who took in Queen Elisabeth (mother of Ladislaus Posthumus) with all her retinue (see p. 104).

To the right, and slightly below the statue, there is a notice which reminds one that the Alsbach, the River Als, at one time flowed through Strauchgasse towards the Danube. Walking across the road we shortly reach another square, Am Hof (see p. 124) but this time go straight on until we come to Bognergasse.

Bognergasse

This is the street where the bow- and arrow-makers plied their trade.

The first house of interest is No. 9 with its Art Nouveau angels (The Angel Pharmacy).

Right next to it, No. 7 bore a gruesome sign "The Death's Head". This sign depicted a skull painted on the wall which the archers used as a target when trying out their bows and arrows to show off their skill.

In 1809 a French grenade exploded in the attic of this house, badly wounding a maid. This servant girl had originally joined the family in the cellar when the bombardment began, but could not resist running upstairs to save her scanty belongings. In those days, servants had their living quarters under the roof.

"The Black Camel" at No. 5 is a delicatessen store founded in 1618 and still carrying its old sign. Actually the name refers to the original owner of the house, one Johann Baptist Cameel. A descendant of the Cameel family was the missionary Father Georg Josef Cameel, a pharmacist and botanist, who spent much of his time on the Philippines, where he collected a great many plants. One of them is named after him: the camellia.

House No. 3 bore a most unusual name: "Where the Devil is fighting with the Bowmaker's Wife". Legend tells of a bowmaker called Caspar Bergauer who had a shrew for a wife. Once, when he was lamenting his fate, the devil appeared and made a wager with him that he would tame this virago. Bergauer was only too pleased to accept and off went the devil to try his luck, not forgetting to take on the outer appearance of the bowmaker. No sooner had he come in at the door than Mrs. Bergauer gave him a good hiding and, to top it off, she threw a jug of cold water over him. This had an unexpected result, for the devil showed himself in his true form. But instead of frightening the woman, it merely enraged her even more and she threw herself at him. Poor Satan, he was no match for this fury. He tried to defend himself as best he could, but when she tore out one of his horns, he deemed it high time to beat at retreat, which he hastily did by way of the chimney.

For many years the house bore the following verse:

> Pestilence and need
> Are evil indeed
> And in war you will forfeit your life.
> But worse than the spite,
> That's the devil's delight
> Is–God help us–a shrew for a wife.

Graben

At the end of Bognergasse we turn right and though this is usually a pretty busy corner, let us try to pause here and look up, up and up, to the very top of the house at the corner of Graben and Kohlmarkt. At a dizzying height you will see the statue of a hussar on a horse. One wonders what he is doing up there; the explanation is rather disappointing. In the 19th century, there was a shop dealing in travel commodities and fire arms. It went by the name "The Hussar". The Viennese, always eager for more romantic versions, claim that it is Johann Sobieski, the Polish King who came to their rescue during the Second Turkish Siege. He is up that high, they say, because from there he can see the foothills of the Kahlenberg, where he won his famous victory.

The house next door, No. 16, stands on the site of one which was a well-known inn where Lord Nelson and Lady Hamilton stayed in 1800.

Before we go on, just a few words in general about Graben and its name. It was the moat of the Roman camp and again used as such during medieval times. It was filled in under Leopold VI, the Glorious, to incorporate numerous villages that had meanwhile accumulated outside the town wall. For the purpose of levelling the town moat, they used part of the ransom paid for Richard Coeur de Lion of England.

For many years it was the site of various markets: flour, bread, meat, vegetables and, around 1600, even the Christmas Market was held here. Under Maria Theresa and Joseph II it was already considered the most elegant shopping street in town. During the summer, there were lemonade and ice-cream booths, which put out chairs for their clients. Thus it became the custom to sit and drink lemonade or almond milk while watching a parade of well-dressed citizens stroll up and down until late into the night. Naturally this much-frequented area proved an ideal hunting ground for the members of the world's oldest profession and these ladies soon acquired the nickname "Graben nymphs".

Roughly in the centre of Graben there is a most spectacular column curving up to the Trinity at the top. It is the memorial Leopold I vowed to erect when the plague subsided. At first only a wooden column was built, but it was replaced by the present monument in 1693. Soon it became the prototype for similar constructions all over Austria. The two fountains to the left and right of this

Pestsäule are dedicated to St. Joseph and St. Leopold (patron saint of Lower Austria).

On the left side of Graben (No. 29), a small street branches off. It is called Trattnerhof in memory of one Trattner, who came to Vienna as a young printer without a penny to his name. He fell in love with a pretty countess who lived on Graben but it seems that she turned him down rather rudely, deeply hurting his feelings. He soon became both rich and influential and, when his wife died–for he had meanwhile married–the countess, who was still single, let him know that she would not be averse to his courting now. He had meanwhile built a fine mansion just opposite his former love's house and, by way of answer, he had a statue erected outside his door which unmistakably and suggestively turned its back on the lady whose windows opened on to the street.

The shop at No. 13, Knize, is one of the few Adolf Loos creations still almost exactly as he designed it. The staircase within, as well as the furnishings, are the originals, only the chandelier upstairs is a reconstruction.

The last point of interest is No. 11 on the other side, but it can best be seen from the left-hand pavement. It is the only Baroque building remaining on Graben and was built in 1720. At that time it was the Palais Bertolotti. Only the fourth floor has been added, otherwise it is a reminder of what Graben must have looked like in the 18th century.

And so we return once more to St. Stephen's Square.

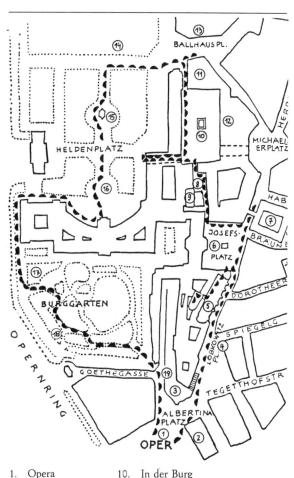

1. Opera
2. Sacher Hotel
3. Albertina
4. Lobkowitzplatz
5. St. Augustine's
6. Josefsplatz
7. Stallburg (Stables)
8. Schweizerhof
9. Burgkapelle
   (Palace Chapel)
10. In der Burg
11. Amalienburg
12. Reichskanzleitrakt
13. Ballhausplatz
14. Volksgarten
15. Statue of Archduke Charles
16. Statue of Prince Eugene
17. Burggarten (Palace Gardens)
18. Statue of Emperor Francis Joseph
19. Statue of Abraham a Santa Clara

SIXTH TOUR

The Opera
Philharmonikerstrasse
Albertinaplatz
Lobkowitzplatz
Augustinerstrasse
Josefsplatz
Stallburg
Hofburg
Schweizerhof
In der Burg
Ballhausplatz
Volksgarten
Heldenplatz
Burggarten

The Opera

This time we will start our tour in front of the Opera, for though St. Stephen's may be the heart of Vienna, the Opera is no doubt its soul.

It is a building consisting of elements taken from various historic styles and the two architects, Siccardsburg and van der Null, came in for much criticism because of it. They were accused, among other things, of having no style of their own and when it was rumoured that even the Emperor did not care for the new Opera, van der Null committed suicide and within a few months Siccardsburg died of a heart attack–"a broken heart", it was said.

But let us not quibble about the outer appearance, for that is not what has made the Vienna Opera what it is to-day. The singers and conductors of world renown, who have contributed to its fame, are legion. I feel completely inadequate in trying to do its fame justice; let it suffice to say that when it was destroyed by bombs, in March 1945, this was a blow that struck the Viennese at their most vulnerable. In the course of a recent television documentary, an eyewitness was asked to describe that scene. He had run out of his nearby shop to see the building ablaze with the roof caved in–and I shall never forget that man, for after no less than forty years, the memory of that moment was still so vivid in his mind, that he covered his face, unable to continue with his story: he wept. Those tears, to me, spoke more vividly than the glib details others were able to contribute.

After a ten-year reconstruction period, when the last Occupation Forces had left Austria, the Opera's re-opening night was an unforgettable occasion for rejoicing, not only for the Viennese, but for the entire country. Beethoven's "Fidelio" had been chosen–a heart-felt expression of liberty regained at last. Loudspeakers broadcast the music in the streets and I was one of those who participated, standing in the crowd by the fountain underneath the Albertina, behind the Opera. I remember a young man sitting on the rim of the fountain, holding the

score and conducting, completely oblivious of his sur-
roundings.

Standing in front of the Opera, your back to the Ring,
turn to the right towards Kärntner Strasse and walk
around the building. Under the arcades towards the
back, there is a small door–"the Stage Door". How
many fans have waited, and still do wait, here to catch a
glimpse of famous opera stars! The corresponding doorway on the opposite side, on Operngasse, is where the
daily tours of the Opera start; opera and theatre fans will
need no urging to participate in one of these.

Thus we arrive at Philharmonikerstrasse and turn left
into it.

Philharmonikerstrasse

The street owes its name to the world-famous Vienna
Philharmonic Orchestra and its location reminds us of
the fact that its members also play at the Opera.

Across from the Opera, stands the renowed Hotel
Sacher. Eduard Sacher, son of a tavern keeper, started
his career as kitchen boy with Prince Schwarzenberg. After his apprenticeship, he travelled abroad and on his return opened a delicatessen store on Kärntner Strasse. He
married Anna, the daughter of a well-to-do butcher. The
two worked so hard that very soon they were able to
build a hotel across the street from their shop. This hotel
soon gained such a reputation that everybody who was
anybody frequented it. One of the main attractions was
the unique Mrs. Sacher herself, who ran the place single-
handed after the death of her husband in 1892. She
would sway her scepter, smoking cigars and giving orders in that deep voice of hers. Her guests held her in
great respect–even archdukes and ministers of state
could not afford to offend her.

In her house the greatest politicans of the day met, so to

speak on neutral ground. Decisions of universal importance were felled, while the chambres séparées discreetly
shut their doors on the love-life of many a prince of
royal blood, or heir to the family fortune of the country's
aristocracy. The menu which Crown Prince Rudolph ordered in his own handwriting, a few days before he committed suicide at Mayerling, still exists. And one of the
scandals that took some time to die down, was when
dizzy young Archduke Otto came down the stairs of the
Sacher, clad only in his sword!

There are endless stories about this hotel; books, plays,
films and even a ballet are based on the subject. This is
perhaps why, even in this age of stream-lined mass-tour-
ism, such a relatively small hotel can still hold its own,
due to the very Viennese atmosphere it offers.

We walk to the other end of Philharmonikerstrasse until
we reach a wide square, Albertinaplatz.

Albertinaplatz

At its further end, this square is closed off by a high
ramp, remnant of the old town wall. A large mansion
rises above it. It is the Albertina. Built in the middle of
the 18th century, but undergoing a series of changes in
the following hundred years, it now houses the world-famous collection of graphic arts started by Albert von
Sachsen-Teschen. Moreover, the papyrus and music collection of the National Library, as well as the Austrian
Film Museum, are incorporated in this building.

The Albertina is the last outpost of the Hofburg complex. All the buildings on that side, including St. Augustine's Church, are connected and I once had the unique
experience of accompanying the Hofburg fire-guard on
his rounds. He has to walk the entire length of the Palace attics from the Amalienburg to the Albertina and
from the Michaeler Gate to the National Library. The

view from up there is breathtaking, but I must admit that in more than one place my knees felt rather weak, as for instance standing behind the golden eagle that crowns the new building of the National Library on Heldenplatz.

But back to Albertinaplatz. From the end of Philharmonikerstrasse we have a fine view of the tower of St. Augustine's and it would therefore be best to give you the story connected with its clock while you can admire it.

This clock was a present from Count Nádasdy who used to live in the house across from the church. He wanted to be able to see what time it was by looking out of his window. Unfortunately, he never did get to reap the reward of his generosity because he was beheaded for high treason in 1670. For a while after his gruesome execution (see p. 114), the Augustinian monks had qualms about accepting his gift, however, they finally overcame their scruples and the clock was mounted on the tower in 1713.

Opposite the Albertina, where there is now a small park, there used to be a large building: the Philipphof. On March 3, 1945 bombs destroyed it completely and hundreds of people who had taken refuge in its air-raid shelters lost their lives. They are still buried there–an inscription, almost overgrown by bushes, has been set up to commemorate their fate.

Let us walk toward the church tower, crossing the square, until we reach Lobkowitzplatz.

Lobkowitzplatz

At one time this square was the pig market, but also a place of execution. It was here that Konrad Vorlauf (see p. 13) and his comrades Rampersdorffer and Rockh were beheaded on July 11, 1408. Theirs is indeed a tragic story:

After the death of Albrecht IV, a feud arose between Leopold IV and Ernest the Iron, as to which of them should act as regent for their under-age cousin Albrecht (later V). Vorlauf, at that time Mayor of Vienna, opposed Leopold who was trying to levy taxes in the city to finance his cause. Thereupon, Leopold had him and his fellow counsellors arrested and later put to death.

When the men were led to the scaffold, Vorlauf is said to have insisted on being the first to die, exclaiming: "Let me be your leader in death as I was in life."

There is a plaque at the corner of Lobkowitzplatz and Gluckgasse commemorating this incident: "... They were victims of their devotion to duty by resisting the unfair demands of Duke Leopold IV."

The palace on the left–no doubt one of the most beautiful examples of Baroque architecture in the city–was originally built for Count Dietrichstein. Its imposing entrance, added later, was designed by Johann Bernhard Fischer von Erlach. In 1783, it passed into the hands of Prince Lobkowitz. Under the auspices of this family, the palace became famous as a music centre. Beethoven performed many of his works in the resplendent Marmorsaal (Marble Hall), with its ornamental frescoed ceiling. His Third Symphony, the Eroica, was first heard within these walls.

At the time of writing, the palais is being renovated and is to become the home of the Theatre Museum.

But now let us return to the corner and turn into Augustinerstrasse.

Augustinerstrasse

The church and monastery belonging to the monks of St. Augustine are on our left. They are now entirely hemmed in by buildings–on the one hand the Hofburg, on the other the Albertina.

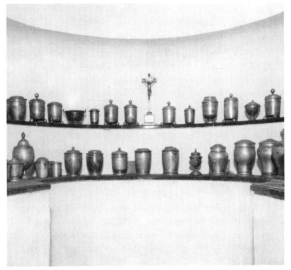

The Habsburg heart urns at St. Augustine's

The church was founded by Frederick the Handsome in the 14th century. It is famous for the Herzgrüftl where the hearts of all the Habsburgs, from Ferdinand II to Maria Theresa, rest in silver containers. When you come to think of it, it is really a rather unpleasant idea that upon their decease the Habsburgs were literally taken to pieces. It seems that different churches laid claim to the honour of being their last resting place. Thus, in most cases, their hearts are to be found at Augustinerkirche–it was, after all, the official parish church of the Court– their entrails at St. Stephen's and their bodies in the Kapuzinergruft (see p. 53).

As the Court Parish Church, the Augustinerkirche was also the scene of many a royal wedding: for instance Maria Theresa and Franz Stephan in 1736 and the last of them, Franz Joseph and Elisabeth in 1854.

The Herzgrüftl is usually only shown to visitors after the

nine o'clock mass in the Loreto Chapel. Next to it is the St. George's Chapel, which from 1337 onwards served as the meeting place of the Knights of St. George, an order founded by Duke Otto the Joyous. Later, the ceremonies in which the Golden Fleece was conferred, were held here. Today it is no longer used as a chapel, but there are some beautiful tombs in it, such as that of Emperor Leopold II, and that of the victor of Kolin, Count Daun. This chapel is only shown at special request.

In the main church, you will find a very famous tomb by the sculptor Antonio Canova. It is that of the Archduchess Maria Christina, wife of Duke Albert of Sachsen-Teschen and favourite daughter of Maria Theresa. A strange procession of mourners is walking into the open tomb to bewail Albert's "best of wives", as the inscription calls her. But she is not actually buried there, she lies with the rest of her family in the Kapuzinergruft.

Walking out of the main entrance of the church we find ourselves on Josefsplatz.

Josefsplatz

It was the great reformer Joseph II who had an old wall torn down, thus opening the space in front of the library. He converted it into a public square, which is named after him. It is also his statue, showing him as a Roman emperor, that stands in the centre.

Doubtless this is one of the most imposing and beautiful squares of the City, flanked by the National Library built by the two Fischers von Erlach, father and son (1721–35) and the Winter Riding School ahead of us.

The main point of focus here is, of course, the central building of the National Library. The goddess of wisdom, Minerva, in her chariot, subjugating envy and ignorance, crowns the roof over the main entrance, which is no longer used today. Originally, the ground floor was

The National Library

destined for the riding school, but later used as carriage houses for Court vehicles. "Horses downstairs, books upstairs" seemed a perfectly legitimate division at that time.

Originally built to house the Habsburg accumulation of books, Charles VI intended the library for "public" use, though until well into the 19th century this meant "scholars only". An American television commentator once quipped that the Habsburgs built a splendid library for themselves, though they were more or less illiterate. Although this may be witty, it is devoid of truth.

From the core of about 80,000 volumes, the library grew and was to incorporate such additions as 15,000 books inherited from Prince Eugene, and the entire libraries of the monasteries dissolved by Joseph II. Today the Fischer von Erlach hall holds approximately 200,000 books.

This hall is surely one of the wonders of Vienna–and certainly an excellent place to get an idea of the essence of the Baroque spirit: light, colour, vitality, gilt and elaboration. Yet here it is all tempered by the magnificence of those thousands of leatherbound volumes, a symphony in brown and gold. The globes, the vibrant statues, the Daniel Gran ceiling, all enhance an already stately hall, but it is the books, those thousands of books that give it this unique atmosphere.

Back in the square, facing the library, you will see two palaces, the Palffy (No. 6) and the Pallavicini (No. 5). The Palffy, the older of the two, was badly damaged in the last war and today shows us a rather austere exterior. It is now used as a cultural centre and one can attend lectures, exhibitions and concerts in some of the halls. The Figarosaal was, as the name implies, both the site of a concert in which Mozart played as a boy and later, in 1786, he is supposed to have given a performance of his "Marriage of Figaro" here for a small circle of friends, prior to its premiere at the nearby Court Theatre.

The Pallavicini was once part of the Queen's Convent (see p. 138) and after its dissolution, the present palace was constructed at the end of the 18th century. It still belongs to the Pallavicini family and is a private residence. Nevertheless, the door is usually open, so let us go in and take a brief look at the grand entrance hall and staircase: both are a good example of the splendour of those old aristocratic mansions. In the summer there are concerts in the festive hall upstairs and, should you be in town at that time, try to attend one as it is an occasion not to be missed.

At the corner of this Palais, we cross Bräunerstrasse, where on an afternoon or evening you are likely to see groups of young people standing around; they are attending a famous dancing school next door. Apart from the usual ballroom dancing, these youngsters will learn first and foremost to master the intricacies of the Viennese waltz.

Stallburg

Entering the arcade, we come to a Renaissance court visible through the large windows on our right. This is the Stallburg, the imperial stables, originally built as a residence for Maximilian II while he was still merely King of Bohemia. But he only lived here briefly. Thus the building came to be used as stables and today it is the home of the famous white horses (Lipizzaner) of the Spanish Riding School. Though these stables are not open to visitors, if you are in luck you may just catch a glimpse of the white horses being led to their morning exercise. Should you have been unable to obtain a ticket to one of the performances, a visit to the training sessions on weekday mornings (check their schedule) is rewarding, as it is most enjoyable to watch these graceful animals being put through their paces.

But from very early on, the Stallburg was also used as a picture gallery. Archduke Leopold Wilhelm was a great collector and when he returned to Vienna after having been Governor of the Spanish Netherlands, he was looking for a place where he could keep the many paintings and other works of art he had accumulated. What had started out as the private collection of an art lover, had meanwhile become one of the greatest art museums in the world. The need to expand by the 19th century resulted in the Art History Museum on the Ring. Yet even this huge building has not been able to accommodate all its treasures and, therefore, the gallery in the Stallburg was reactivated once again and, whereas the Art Mu-

The white horses of the Spanish Riding School

seum is the home of the famous Brueghels, the Veláz-
quez and Rubens, this little "New Gallery" can boast of
Corots, Böcklins, Renoirs, Degas, Manets and many
more.

The courtyard, however, has another attraction: the
lovely wrought-iron well which, at one time had stood in
front of the Amalienburg in the inner court of the Palace,
now graces it. And before moving on, do look up at the
roof at the very tall, typically Renaissance chimneys
which have a charm of their own.

A bit further on the Old Court pharmacy still dispenses
prescriptions. A glimpse into its interior is fascinating.
Apart from the two hundred-year-old clock over the
door at the back, the apothecary's scales, brass mortars
and pestles, a Latin inscription informs us that "Maria
Theresa, Austrian Majesty, and Francis the First ordered
the establishment and equipment of this pharmacy for
domestic and public use in the year 1746".

Leaving the old pharmacy, let us cross the road to the

door through which the horses are taken to their training sessions and performances. Let us, however, head back to Josefsplatz. Under the arches there are windows with photographs of the Spanish Riding School, as well as a saddle and other pertinent requisites.

On reaching the square turn right, walk to the far end, past the entrance of the Riding School and the Redoutensaal, finally ending up in the right-hand corner. It is here, through an inconspicuous passage, rather than through the 19th century Michaelertor, that I would like to take you into the Hofburg, the Imperial Town Palace of the Habsburg Dynasty.

Hofburg

There is method in my madness, for by taking you in, by the back entrance as it were, the tradesmen's entrance, which indeed it used to be, I can bring you to the core, the nucleus of the Palace in an endeavour to acquaint you with it chronologically–a difficult task, as you will soon see.

On entering the passageway from Josefsplatz, your first impression may well be one of dinginess. But don't despair–things improve, for shortly we come to a small courtyard which already has a surprise: to the left we see the Gothic choir of the Burgkapelle (the Palace chapel). Originally, the moat enclosing the self-contained medieval castle with its four corner towers ran along here. It must have been pretty deep for the chapel reached far down into it. You can just see the ornaments which topped another row of windows; these, however, are no longer visible since the moat was filled in and the courtyard paved.

This moat was also presumably the scene of Kronberger's daring venture to come to the rescue when Frederick III was besieged in the castle. The hole through which he is supposed to have been hauled into the building, can still be seen between the chapel wall and the window on the fourth floor (for the entire story, see p. 102).

Still heading straight on we again pass through another "tunnel". To the right is a small door leading to a staircase called the "Zehrgadenstiege". It was here that food supplies for the Court were delivered and stored. If you go inside and look up into the stairwell, you can still get some idea of what the ancient corner towers, of which this was one, were like.

Schweizerhof

Next we come into the Schweizerhof–the square around which the medieval castle was built. It has changed greatly in the course of the centuries. The chapel is no doubt the oldest part still recognizable as Gothic. The staircase leading up to it was variably called "chapel stairs" or "kitchen stairs", for the kitchen was located directly below. I ought to point out that the name "Swiss Courtyard" is of a much later date, derived from the Swiss mercenary soldiers who kept watch at the gate and its drawbridge.

But back to the chapel. It is open to visitors at specified times and also at mass on Sundays and religious holidays from mid-September to end of June. But the incredible crowds this rather small erstwhile private chapel of the royal family draws are not due merely to either its architectural beauty or its historic significance, but to the fact that the world-famous Vienna Boys' Choir sings there at mass. The beginnings of this choir go back to the days of Emperor Maximilian I, though there was some semblance of a choir and orchestra of Court musicians even prior to this time. When Ferdinand II became Emperor, Vienna finally came into its own as an Imperial City, for henceforth it was the seat of the Royal Court and thus a permanent Court orchestra and choir became feasible. This institution gained in importance under the "composer emperors" Ferdinand III, Leopold I, Joseph I and Charles IV. Apart from performing the truly "royal" music of these monarchs, the Court musicians attracted some of the most famous composers: Haydn, Mozart, Schubert and Bruckner were all closely connected with them.

Today the Hofmusikkapelle consists of members of the State Opera Orchestra and the Vienna Boys' Choir. This choir has meanwhile been divided into four sections of twenty-four choristers each and has proved to be the one Austrian "export" which is always in demand the world over.

As practically every tourist includes a visit to the Vienna Boys' Choir in his schedule, I think I ought to clarify what such a visit will offer you in order to spare you unnecessary disappointment. You will be attending a Roman Catholic mass, in other words a religious ceremony; this is therefore not a concert. Accordingly, the choir boys and musicians are up in the organ loft and can only be seen by means of video screens down below. Perhaps I ought to mention that in adherence to ancient tradition, the choir sings a cappella, that is, unaccompanied by the orchestra, during Lent.

As I have already mentioned, there are tours of the chapel (see annex) and it certainly merits a visit for its own sake. At one time both the walls and the ceiling were painted. Of this glory only a very small remnant may be seen on the second floor, next to the organ loft. From the left side altar one of the "beautiful" Virgins, dating back to about 1410, looks down at us. Behind the main altar, a row of magnificent statues has been preserved. Most of them are auxiliary saints, but there is also an annunciation scene–a Virgin and angel, the latter, however, seems to have mislaid his wings. Behind this angel, you can also still see the painted curtain that was once the background of all the saints.

Another remarkable feature of this chapel is the diversity

The Angel Gabriel in the Royal Court Chapel

and artistry of the bosses, or sculptured stone knobs hanging from the rib junctions of the vaulting.

Do look a little closer at the small wooden crucifix on the main altar; there is a story connected with it. Ferdinand II has gone down in history as the fanatical defender of the Roman Catholic faith in the face of the turbulent days of the Reformation. When the Thirty Years' War broke out, his advisers tried to persuade him to leave Vienna, but he refused. When the Protestant army stood at the gates of the city, all hope seemed to dwindle. Ferdinand had no army, no money and he could not even count on the Viennese to defend him. In this drastic situation he went to the chapel to pray and as he knelt before the crucifix he distinctly heard it say to him:

"Ferdinand, I shall not desert you." A few days later the Emperor was besieged in his own castle. A delegation of Austrian Protestants tried to make him concede to their demands. The argument became very heated and irreverent shouts of "Ferdy, go on and sign!" and "Nando, give up!" were heard, but Ferdinand stood firm. Suddenly there was a great commotion: the blare of trumpets and clatter of horses down in the courtyard. A cavalry regiment had arrived, sent by the Emperor's brother Leopold and thus Ferdinand was saved at the last minute.

But let us leave the chapel and return to the Schweizerhof. In the corner to the left of the chapel, on the ground floor, the Treasury has recently been re-opened. Personally I think that a visit to this unique collection of Imperial Crown Jewels and other Habsburg treasures is a must. Let me merely mention a few of its most famous exhibits to whet your appetite: the 10th century octagonal crown, the "bursa" of St. Stephen, the so-called sabre of Charlemagne, the Holy Lance, orbs and sceptres and crowns of the "Holy Roman Empire" and the "Austrian Empire", but also reminders of bygone splendours, such as coronation robes, baptismal garments, heralds' tunics, beautifully embroidered, as well as the Order of the Golden Fleece. There is the silver cradle of the Duke of Reichstadt, Napoleon's son; priceless tapestries line the walls and such curios as the "unicorn" or the agate bowl give an added flair of the unusual, to say nothing of the wealth of the ecclesiastic treasury. Have I said enough? I could go on and on, but if I have been unable to arouse your interest, let us continue our walk.

Our next stop is the imposing red, black and gold Renaissance gate leading into the Inner Square of the Palace. This splendid archway was the work of the painter and stonemason Pietro Ferrabosco. It has the year of its completion, 1553, inscribed on it. To the right there is the lovely fountain with its wrought-iron railing, also attributed to this artist.

Before we enter the gate, do cast a brief glance at the "Diplomats' Staircase" to your left. A pretty story is connected with it. When it became obvious that Joseph II

The Swiss Gate

would leave no male heir, he sent for his nephew Francis, his brother Leopold's son, to give him the education befitting a future emperor. When Francis arrived in Vienna and the carriage drew up at the bottom of this staircase, he is supposed to have turned to his coachman with the words: "John, no more fun and games–as of tomorrow I'll be apprenticed to an emperor."

Let me finally draw your attention to a strange inscription. It is on one of the black stones, about two-and-a-half feet from the ground on the left side of the gate and reads: "Si deus pro nobis quis contra nos" (If God is with us, who can oppose us?). Who wrote this sentence and on what occasion? This seems to be an unsolved mystery and, so far, I have been unable to find a satisfactory solution. There are two different versions: one is that it was the Protestants besieging Ferdinand who scribbled it in the stone. The other claims that it was Leopold I who, upon returning to Vienna after the Turkish Siege, in the presence of the entire Court, ceremoniously carved it on the gate to celebrate his homecoming. The third explanation that has been put forward was that it is connected with the Thirty Years' War. The date 1660 after the inscription, however, contradicts all these interpretations, though their advocates claim that this date was added later.

Directly opposite this enigmatic inscription, on the right side of the gate, is another one, which to most people must seem equally mysterious. It reads: "Restaur. in memoriam Caroli Altmann 1949" and is the touching memorial dedicated by a son to his father.

Bernhard Altmann, the son, had been forced to emigrate when Hitler entered Austria. He made a new home for himself and his family in the United States, but after the war he returned to Vienna and re-established his textile business. It was as a secretary in this company that I had the privilege of getting to know this "grand old man", an entrepreneur of the old school, as well as a patron of the arts. He has described what prompted him to donate a very generous sum for the restoration of the Schweizertor better than I can and, therefore, I prefer to quote from his memoirs: "When I was about six years old, my father took me and my sister to see the Easter Parade in the inner courtyard of the Palace. There this kind-hearted man stood in front of the so-called Swiss Gate, the oldest part of the Palace, and carried me and my sister on his shoulders for two hours. I shall never forget what my good father did for us children.

When I returned to Vienna in 1949 and found that the Swiss Gate was in a deplorable state I had it restored in memory of my father and it bears the inscription 'in memoriam Caroli Altmann' to this day."

Walking through this magnificent arch we can admire its painted ceiling depicting the various coats-of-arms belonging to the Austrian domains over which Ferdinand ruled.

In der Burg

On the other side we come out into the square which, today, is called "In der Burg" or Inner Palace Court. To the left and right of the gate you can still see the moat and are in fact walking over what was a drawbridge. Turning once more to admire the gate, you can make out the winches used hoist this bridge. Above an elaborate frieze of animal skulls, flower garlands etc., the central shield on the gate shows the coats-of-arms of Ferdinand's territories and the inscription names his titles: "Ferdinand, Holy Roman Emperor, King of Hungary and Bohemia, Infante of Spain, Archduke of Austria, Duke of Burgundy 1552".

Once again we are in a square of unique fascination–and it is strange that the conglomeration of so many different styles should provide such a harmonious result. With our back to the Swiss Gate, let us look around us: directly in front, in the centre of the square, is the statue of Francis (the II. as Holy Roman Emperor and the I. as Austrian Emperor). On its pedestal we find the words "Amorem meum populis meis" (My love to my people). As the Monarch was known to have been pretty tight-fisted, someone had scathingly commented: "Yes, his love, but nothing else, not even a single penny for the poor."

The Amalia Wing with its clocks and the "Palace Horsey"

Across the square is the late 16th century Amalienburg which Maximilian II had originally built for his son Rudolph and it was, therefore, at first known as the Rudolphinian Wing. But when Rudolph acceeded to the throne he did not find Vienna much to his liking and betook himself and his Court to Prague. The name this wing now bears goes back to Wilhelmina Amalia, widow of Joseph I. She made it her home and died here in 1742. The Amalienburg also reminds us that though Rudolph II never resided there, he did engage several well-known artists to work on the completion of the building. No doubt Rudolph's interest in astronomy, alchemy and magic, as well as his close association with the renowned astronomer Tycho Brahe, are partly responsible for the sundial and the "lunar clock", a most unusual timepiece showing the phases of the moon.

At the top there is a pretty belfry with green patina. If you look closely you may just be able to make out a weather vane in the shape of a horse. This "Palace Horsey" as it was called, used to be consulted by many Viennese in lieu of a weather forecast. Even Empress Elisabeth is supposed to have set great store by the predictions of the "Palace Horsey" before she went out riding. The unhappy Empress inhabited rooms on the first floor and these, together with those belonging to her husband Franz Joseph, are open to the public (see annex). Poor Elisabeth, wife of the man who ruled one of the greatest empires, she felt hemmed in on all sides. Her mother-in-law made her life at Court a misery and saw to it that her children grew up as strangers. Thus the Empress finally took refuge in ill-health and travel. She spent most of her married life away from her husband and family. Much has been written about Elisabeth, but she still remains something of an enigma. We do know that she loved riding and was extremely weight-conscious; in her bedroom you can still see the implements for her daily workout. Such an unladylike pastime would have been frowned upon where any woman of her day was concerned, let alone the Empress of Austria. She also had what must have seemed downright revolutionary ideas on personal hygiene, for she had a W.C. and bathroom installed in her apartments–the first in the entire Palace.

The wing on the right, the "Reichskanzleitrakt" is the work of the younger Fischer von Erlach and a truly regal residence. It is in this building that Franz Joseph's imperial apartments are located. If you take the guided tour you will perhaps be struck by the fact that among all this splendour, the rooms exude a certain lack of personality. Has every trace of it been purposely removed or did the

Emperor, who liked to consider himself merely as the foremost civil servant, suppress any such uncalled-for individualism, sacrificing it in favour of duty? What little is left of any hint of their private lives tends to shock us: the narrow army cot Franz Joseph slept on–and the nun-like iron bedstead of his spouse in the other wing . . .

I also find it surprising that the Emperor's bedroom features only scenes of battles, though by nature he was hardly of a warlike disposition. Did his battle-axe of a mother have a say in this choice? His wife's bedroom, on the other hand, is studded with portraits of her favourite horses.

The tour also shows the imperial dinner table, laid for a meal. These dinners were much feared by those invited, because the Emperor was both a poor and a fast eater. Of course he was always served first and by the time the last person at the table had been served, the Emperor had finished. The strict etiquette at Court forbade anyone to eat after the Emperor had laid down his knife and fork, so many a guest rose from the imperial table as hungry as he had sat down. It was standard procedure to go straight from the Palace to Mrs. Sacher's for a decent meal after an invitation to sup with the Emperor.

The last wing to our left is the Leopoldinische Trakt. From this side it is rather a comedown after the others, being the reverse side of what we shall later discover is a handsome edifice where it faces Heldenplatz.

If we now turn left there is a triple passage which leads to this "Heroes' Square". The central lane is for traffic, the two side ones for pedestrians. I would like to take you into the left one first. Today it has several shops, but on the inside, on the right wall, part of the plaster has been scraped off and beneath it we see the original stone wall of the Widmer Tor which, as the sign next to it explains, was the ancient town gate located next to one of the four corner towers of the old castle fortress. The gate itself was part of the town fortifications from the 13th to the beginning of the 16th century.

A little further on a staircase behind an iron gate leads up to the offices of the Water Preservation Agency. These stairs were once referred to as the "Beggars' Staircase" because it led to the "Controllers' Corridor". In the days of Joseph II this corridor passed close to the Emperor's bedroom and on certain days he would receive anyone who had some kind of grievance or request. People from all walks of life are supposed to have come and the Emperor tried to deal fairly with their petitions. He asked each one three questions: "Who are you? What do you want? Have you got it in writing?" Innumerable stories circulated about the wise and enlightened Monarch, one of which was that an impoverished aristocratic widow came to ask what would become of her daughter who was penniless and without a dowry. The Emperor's advice was: "Let her serve." The lady was horrified: "Serve?" "Yes, why not?" replied the Monarch. "I, the Emperor, also serve you and others continually."

Just beyond this staircase a small door leads to the quarters of the Palace Fire Brigade. The members of this squad make the rounds of the Palace every two hours, day and night, and I have already mentioned my having joined one of them (see p. 168).

We go straight on, however, and shortly find ourselves out on Heldenplatz. But instead of letting you enjoy the view from here, I intend to take you back to the Inner Court via the other pedestrian passage, because there are still a few things to be seen before we return to the square at its further end.

In this passage, and heading back to where we came from, I cannot resist showing you something which strangely moves me every time I see it. These are the wooden beams that separate the pedestrian passage from the street. If you look closely, you will notice that they are full of notches and grooves. These are the original beams where, for centuries, riders and coachmen tethered their horses before entering the Palace.

Upon our return to the Inner Court, immediately adjoining the passage on the left, is one of the old stone sentry boxes. This courtyard was famous for the ceremony of the "changing of the guard" at noon each day. Indeed, the Habsburgs were, with the exception of Joseph II, very much of the opinion, which Empress Maria Theresa voiced so aptly: "Spectacles are indispensible!" And the spectacles that royalty throughout the centuries offered its subjects were innumerable: birthdays, weddings, funerals, parades, religious processions, jubilees–and this courtyard inside the Palace was the scene of many of them.

We continue our walk along the left side of the square and before long arrive at a staircase called the "Zucker-bäckerstiege" (the Confectioners' Stairs). It received its name during the time of Maria Theresa's reign and led to her apartments. One can just imagine her many children crowding around when the confectioners came running up the stairs to the nursery to bring them all sorts of goodies.

In the far corner we come to another staircase, the "La-kaienstiege" (Footmen's Stairs) and to the right of it the "Adlerstiege" (Eagle's Stairs). This latter owes its name to a strange incident. In May of 1706, during the War of the Spanish Succession, Joseph I saw a most unusual sight: an eagle flew into the Inner Court from the West, alighted briefly in the corner by the stairs and then took off again. The Emperor, and those who had witnessed this scene, were convinced that the appearance of an eagle must have some mystical significance and everyone saw these feelings confirmed when a few days later a horseman arrived with the news that Marlborough and Prince Eugene had beaten the French at the Battle of Ramilliers on the very day and at the very hour when the eagle had swooped down into the courtyard. It was, however, his brother Charles who, upon succeeding to the throne, gave this name to the staircase to commemorate the incident.

Ballhausplatz

The square is named after a ball house where badminton was played at one time. Coming from the Hofburg the Federal Chancellor's Office faces us across the road. Johann Lukas von Hildebrandt built it for Charles VI as a court chancellery. Extended under that monarch's daughter, Maria Theresa, it was used as the offices of both interior and foreign affairs–and it still houses the Foreign Ministry as well as the Chancellery.

The famous and much feared Metternich made it his headquarters as Chancellor, until his downfall in the revolutionary year 1848.

It has another gruesome memory as the scene of an assassination. Engelbert Dollfuss, Austrian Chancellor from 1932–34, was murdered in his office here on July 25, 1934. On that day, 154 members of the still illegal SS troopers invaded the Chancellery. To this day, it is not quite clear what happened. Shots ring out, the Chancellor is wounded–yet he tries to argue with the youngsters who accuse him of ruining Austria and "betraying Germany". Dollfuss tries to reason with them, then–as he is wounded–asks for a doctor and a priest. They refuse him both. He finally bleeds to death. Whatever one may think of the man himself–he was after all a dictator–yet he was the first and only statesman in Europe who opposed Hitler at that time.

To our left is the Austrian President's Office, above which the Austrian flag flies when he is "at home". But this projecting building had a different purpose originally. In her latter years, Maria Theresa became increasingly corpulent and, to spare her the stairs of the "Adlerstiege", a ramp was built up to the first floor so that carriages could drive right up to the imperial apartments. This ramp had to go when these were razed to make way for the Ringstrasse. Owing to the "pleasant air" which surrounded this part of the Palace, it was, and still is, called "Bellaria". The street of this same name near the Parliament was once the direct approach leading to the Palace ramp.

Volksgarten

If you now walk across the street, heading for the fence, you will find an entrance to the Volksgarten. Weather permitting, I suggest a pleasant stroll in this park. As soon as you enter the gate, you can see the white statue of the Empress Elisabeth in her arbour at the end of a tree-lined avenue.

Raised in an environment of extraordinary freedom for a young girl of her times, she was a romantic at heart and was never able to adjust to the straight-laced and almost inhuman ceremony of the Imperial Court. She found no happiness either as Empress or as wife, though Franz Joseph adored her till the day he died. And as she was denied the normal joys of motherhood—her children were separated from her practically at birth—she could not find any solace in their company either. All these circumstances combined to make her life a burden. Apart from this she had to face tragedy within the family twice. Her daughter Sophie died at the age of only two and later there was, of course, the horror of her son Rudolph's "suicide". Her own terrible end at the hands of a political maniac shocked all of Europe, but seemed in consistency with her entire life.

From her memorial it is only a few steps to the left before we reach the exit. If you would care to make a short detour for a closer inspection of the Burgtheater (Court Theatre) and the Rathaus, this is where you should leave the park. But I suggest we turn back into the Volksgarten. During the summer months its rose garden is a delightful place to linger.

Back in the direction of Heldenplatz, we come rather unexpectedly upon a Grecian temple, nowadays a favourite trysting place of the young generation. The temple itself is a 19th century copy of the Athenian Theseus Temple.

A few steps further on you will find a pleasant out-door café, open only in the summer months, where a snack or cool drink might revive you for further ventures.

Heldenplatz

We leave the Volksgarten by the exit that leads directly towards the equestrian statue of Archduke Charles. This statue is surrounded by lilacbushes and, to my mind, it is one of the most beautiful spots in the city when, in May, these are in full bloom, to say nothing of the fragrance that envelopes you if you sit on one of the benches.

It is also a splendid vantage point for admiring the Leopold Wing of the Hofburg, for here it presents itself in its full glory.

This Leopold I was an extraordinary personality. As he was not originally intended as heir to the throne and only succeeded because his brother Ferdinand died so young, he was unprepared and most unhappy at the burden which he had to shoulder. He was a gifted musician, played the flute very well, was a composer in his own right and often conducted the Court orchestra and choirboys. He also sponsored performances of other composers and on the occasion of his wedding, had a theatre built specially for the production of "Il Pomo d'Oro", the first opera to be performed in Vienna.

He, like Maria Theresa at a later date, was very much in favour of any kind of spectacle, preferably one in which he was personally involved. He participated in opera performances and pageants, led the equestrian ballets himself—and therefore presented the ever eager Viennese audiences with plenty of entertainment.

Being a patron of the arts naturally also influenced the construction of the wing named after him. It took seven years to build, but only a few months after its completion a fire broke out and destroyed it. Though the Imperial Family escaped unscathed, others suffered considerably. These were the Viennese Jews, for someone had spread the rumour that they were to blame for the arson. The Empress herself, only 17 at the time, was only too eager to support this view. She had been brought up at the bigoted Roman Catholic Court of Spain and before coming to Vienna had made a vow to expel the Jews from the city. Leopold, rather unwillingly, finally agreed to abolish the ghetto and banish the Jews. Leopold's Wing was later inhabited by both Maria Theresa and her son Joseph II. For many years the rooms they occupied were open to the public, but since the President of Austria now presides in the very room which served as Joseph's office, they are no longer on display.

Before leaving, please do not forget to pay your respects to the horse and rider immediately before you. Apart from being a tribute to the Austrian hero of the Napoleonic Wars, Archduke Charles, it is unique: the horse is standing on its hinds legs only, without support from the tail or one of the forelegs, as is the case in all other equestrian statues the world over. Even the sculptor who created this marvel, Fernkorn, was unable to duplicate it. Its counterpart, the statue of Prince Eugene on the other side of Heldenplatz, though perfectly acceptable as far as statues go, cannot match it with regard to equilibrium. Being unable to repeat his former success is supposed to have driven Fernkorn mad, or was it the beginnings of insanity that are to blame for his failure?

But it is time to move on again. Let us cross this monumental square–its very dimensions are heroic–and steer towards this other horseman: Prince Eugene, the Noble Knight, as he is called. He served no less than three Austrian emperors: as a young unknown officer, under Leopold I, he made a name for himself in the Turkish Siege; his career was meteoric, for less than 15 years later he was driving the Turk out of Europe as a general. Under Joseph I he fought side by side with the Duke of Marlborough in the War of the Spanish Succession and finally ended his life as a statesman and diplomat under Charles VI.

Behind the rearing horse with its gallant rider is the reading room of the National Library. Moreover, this 19th century addition also contains some of the collections of the Museum of Art: ancients instruments, weapons and armour, as well as the excavations from Ephesos.

Let us walk up the steps to the entrance of the Library, for from here you have a fine view of the entire Heldenplatz. During the reign of Emperor Francis Joseph the palace saw a period of extensive building activity. Apart from the addition of the Michaeler Wing (see p. 141), the palace was to stretch all the way to the Messepalast on this side. The wing behind us, built at the turn of the century, was to have a counterpart on the opposite side by the Volksgarten so that the square would become a closed forum. Luckily this project never materialized; thus we have a wonderful view over part of the city from here and on clear days you can even see as far as the Vienna Woods.

The Burgtor (Palace Gate), the colonnade to your left closing off the square from the Ring, bears Emperor Francis' motto: "Justitia regnorum fundamentum" (Justice is the ground on which kingdoms are built). Today it is a memorial for the victims of Austria's fight for freedom.

To the right, in the corner of the Palace, flags of many nations are flying over the entrance to the Convention Centre. Here international conferences meet all year long. But this wing also houses the large Palace Ballroom in which most of the elite balls of the Vienna carnival take place. Each year the season opens on December 31 with the Emperor's Ball.

But now let us turn towards the Ring and walk past the Ethnological Museum. Rather than go out on to the noisy Ring, I suggest we take the path on the left, on the inside of the fence (though from November 1 to March 1 this is closed, in which case just go out the gate immediately in front, keep left and simply re-enter at the first opportunity). This leads us to the Burggarten (Palace Gardens).

Burggarten

Once the private Palace Gardens, this park is now a very pretty as well as popular one. Straight ahead, if you have come on the inside lane, you will see the statue of Mo-

Emperor Francis Joseph

zart, but to your left there is a lovely view: at the far end of the park, like the set of a gigantic stage, we see the back of the National Library (the old one), the Palace green houses where, not so many years ago, an annual spring flower show used to be held. Once the green-houses have been restored, these flower shows will hopefully be resumed. Behind these is the Albertina, high on its ramp, with the spire of the Augustinerkirche looking over the top.

Let us walk past Mozart, then take the first lane to your left and the very next one to the right. Hidden away among the shrubs is one member of the Habsburg family of whom you have heard much, but with whom you have not as yet come face to face. And even now it is his back you see first: an elderly man in uniform–yes, he wore a uniform all his life, except when he went hunting. Here finally is Francis Joseph, the Emperor who reigned for no less than 68 years. He stands here, an old man, weary after the many trials and tribulations which caused him to say the famous: "Mir bleibt nichts erspart!" (I am spared nothing–or a little more frivolously, Everything happens to me!).

Let us bid the old Kaiser farewell and walk to the left till we get to the green house and then through the gate on our right. Just outside the gate, to your left, is the statue of a monk. It is Abraham a Sancta Clara, a famous 17th century preacher. His witty sermons are still a pleasure to read today. Now we are in Hanuschgasse which takes us straight back to the Opera.

A RIDE AROUND THE RING

(Annex)

The Ring

This time I shall not expect you to walk. I would consider it an imposition. It would take too long and be too tiresome.

So I suggest you take a ride. As I see it, you can choose the vehicle according to your purse: if you have money to spare and the weather is clement, take a "Fiaker" (a horse carriage); if not, a streetcar ticket will take you all the way round the Ring and you can sit back comfortably and admire the sights in every kind of weather.

Presuming that you have opted for the streetcar, there is a stop directly across from the Opera, on the other side of the Ring.

Before you get on, however, let me say just a few words about the Ringstrasse as such. The old town walls, still effective as fortifications during the Turkish Siege of 1683, had outlived their day by the time Napoleon arrived on the scene in 1806 and for the next fifty years or so served merely as Vienna's most popular promenade. Thus the walls were finally razed by imperial command in 1857 and the surrounding suburbs incorporated into the city. A spacious boulevard was then built to encircle the ancient core. All the most important public buildings were to be erected here and the function of each edifice was to be symbolically expressed by its architectural style. The resulting historicism came to be known as the "Ringstrassenstil".

Now, please get on a streetcar No. 2, settle yourself by a window, preferably on the right side–and here we go.

NOTE: As the Ring is a one-way street, should you decide to go by Fiaker, you will have to read this annex in reverse order.

The first two blocks, once the streetcar gets going, are not so very interesting, but be sure to look at the view presented through the streets after the second and third block, for there you can briefly see the magnificent Baroque church of St. Charles. With its green cupola and the two golden-green-topped columns, it is another of the creations of the Fischers von Erlach, father and son. And immediately after it, we come to Schwarzenbergplatz–a large square (seen from afar in the Second Tour p. 50). Just as a quick reminder: it is Prince Schwarzenberg that you see on his horse in the foreground; further back is the fountain and behind it the column with the Russian Unknown Soldier.

But we are fast approaching the next landmark. Soon after leaving the stop at Schwarzenbergplatz we come to the City Park (Stadtpark). At the next stop there is an entrance to this park, but it is not until the streetcar starts up again that we can look into the park–and momentarily catch sight of Johann Strauss, the Waltz King.

For a little while we are running parallel to the park, though from the streetcar we cannot really appreciate its beauty which is mostly hidden by bushes and trees.

To the right of the next stop (Wollzeile) there is the red brick Museum of Applied Arts in the Italian Renaissance style with its sgraffito frieze and adjoining it the Academy of Applied Arts.

And now you must prepare yourself for a quick look to the left where, set slightly back from the Ring, the Otto Wagner Postal Savings Bank comes into view (see p. 81) and immediately to the right again, where the large ornate one-time War Ministry stands behind the equestrian statue of the famous Austrian general Radetzky. The building is now the seat of various ministries such as agriculture, commerce and construction etc.

At the next stop (Julius-Raab-Platz) we can already make out the rather extraordinary Urania observatory building ahead. It was built in 1909/10 by Max Fabiani, one of Otto Wagner's students. Today it also houses two cinemas and an adult education centre.

As the streetcar curves round to the left on to the Kai along the Danube Canal, do look back as soon as you have passed the Urania, for there–in the distance behind the bridge–you can just discern another famous Viennese landmark: the Riesenrad, that Giant Wheel (Ferris Wheel) which was built in 1897 and is still the main attraction of the Prater Fun Fair.

The ride along the Kai is not terribly exciting as one cannot even see the Canal which is below street level, but merely the tops of trees that border its banks. After the Schwedenplatz stop, look towards the left and shortly you will recognize the pretty creeper-covered church of St. Ruprecht (see p. 69).

The streetcar stops at Salztorbrücke and now you can already make out a small, delightful, navy-blue and white building ahead on the far side of the Canal. It is Otto Wagner's "Schützenhaus" (1906/7), originally designed to control a lock on a weir which was never built.

At the next stop (Schottenring), or as the streetcar once more turns left leaving the Kai and entering the Ring, you can perhaps catch a glimpse of what looks like a fortress. And, indeed, the Rossauer Kaserne is supposed to create just that impression. These erstwhile army barracks were built in 1865–69. When finished, it was discovered that the architects had forgotten to include toilets, which caused much scathing comment at the time.

Opposite the next stop (Börse) lies the red brick pseudo-Renaissance palace which is the Stock Exchange. A work of the architect Theophil Hansen, it opened its doors here in 1877.

Brace yourself, for shortly we come to the most interesting part of the Ring and you will be kept very busy turning your head this way and that in quick succession.

Just before we come to the next stop (Schottentor) we get a good view of the double-spired neo-Gothic Votivkirche, a church built to commemorate the near escape of Emperor Francis Joseph when an abortive attempt at assassinating him was made here.

Immediately after leaving this stop, also on the right, we pass the Vienna University which, in accordance with the Ringstrasse Historicism, is naturally Renaissance as a reminder this era was the Age of Learning.

A park follows and above the trees you can already see the tall neo-Gothic tower of the Rathaus (City Hall) with its iron-clad knight on the top–the period it symbolizes saw the rise of the municipality. But when the streetcar comes to a halt, be sure to look to your left where

A RIDE AROUND THE RING

Austria's National Theatre (Burgtheater or Court Theatre) faces the Rathaus, resplendent in pseudo-Baroque.

While from here till the next stop the Volksgarten (see p. 191), borders the Ring to the left and the Rathaus park is to our right, we are fast approaching the Greek parliament building–Greece having been the cradle of democracy–with the goddess of wisdom, Pallas Athene, standing guard in front of it. You may also have a moment to admire the winged charioteers with their prancing horses on the parliament roof.

On the right is the Natural History Museum, shortly followed by the Arts History Museum with the Empress Maria Theresa seated on her throne between them. She is surrounded by her four famous generals on horseback. With all this wealth on your right, should you have time to turn your head briefly–on the other side of the Ring is that columned arch leading to Heldenplatz (see p. 192).

By the way, had you noticed that under the trees there are still two and sometimes three lanes in some places? Seemingly all of them are for pedestrians. Originally, however, one was for horse-riding; recently the City Fathers have reactivated this function, only nowadays it isn't horses but bicycles that are being ridden here.

Next stop, Babenbergerstrasse, conjures up other glamorous memories: it was from here to Heldenplatz that the parade wound its way on the occasion of the silver wedding of Emperor Francis Joseph and Elisabeth. This procession consisted of no less than 10,000 participants, all dressed either in historical or national costume. None other than the famous painter Hans Makart had been commissioned to "orchestrate" this colourful spectacle.

At the end of the park on the left (Burggarten, see p. 194), we see a gentleman seated majestically, even though he is no member of a royal house. The Ring, after all, symbolizes the rise of the bourgeoisie. Yet he *is* a prince, the prince of German literature: Johann Wolfgang von Goethe. But turn quickly and on your right a little further back is his counterpart, standing in front of the Academy of Fine Arts: Friedrich von Schiller.

At the next stop, the Opera, we have come full circle and this is where we get off.

Having arrived at the end of my tours, I would just like to say that obviously they only present a small selection, and a very personal selection at that. A book such as this cannot hope to cover the wealth a city like Vienna has to offer; indeed an entire volume could have been dedicated to each of the walking tours. But this, in turn, would have defeated the original purpose, namely that of being a handy guide to arouse the interest of the tourist and would-be explorer. If I have been able to whet your appetite and should you have the time to go on investigating on your own, I feel I have been more than successful.

As it is, I hope I have at least managed to convey a little of my own love of this city and the delight of my discoveries.

Index of Names

INDEX OF NAMES

Index of Places

INDEX OF PLACES

INDEX OF PLACES

Museums

All information (as of March 1987)
subject to alteration without prior notice

Academy of Fine Arts
1, Schillerplatz 3, phone 58 8 16*0
Tue, Thu, Fri 10 a.m.–2 p.m., Wed
10 a.m.–1 p.m. and 3 p.m.–6 p.m., Sat,
Sun, Holidays 9 a.m.–1 p.m.

Albertina Collection of Graphic Arts
1, Augustinerstrasse 1, phone 534 83
Mon, Tue, Thu 10 a.m.–4 p.m., Wed
10 a.m.–6 p.m., Fri 10 a.m.–1 p.m. July,
August: Sun closed

Chapel of the Imperial Palace
1, Hofburg, Schweizerhof
Guided tours from mid-January till
June and from mid-September till mid-
December, Tue, Thu 2:30–3:30 p.m.
Mass with the Vienna Boys' Choir at
9:15 a.m. on Sundays and religious holi-
days

Clock Museum (Uhrenmuseum)
1, Schulhof 2, phone 63 22 65
Tue–Sun 9 a.m.–12:15 p.m. and
1–4:30 p.m.

Habsburg Heart Urns
in the Church of the Augustinian Friars
1, Augustinerstrasse 3, phone 52 33 38

**Historical Museum of the City of
Vienna**
4, Karlsplatz, phone 65 87 47
Tue–Sun 9 a.m.–4:30 p.m.

Imperial Burial Vault (Kapuzinergruft)
1, Neuer Markt, phone 52 68 53
May–September daily 9:30 a.m.–4 p.m.
October–April daily 9:30 a.m.–1 p.m.

Imperial Palace (Hofburg)
State Rooms, Imperial Apartments
1, Michaelerplatz, phone 587 55 45/515
Mon–Sat 8:30 a.m.–4 p.m., Sun
8:30 a.m.–12:30 p.m.

Mozart Memorial "Figaro House"
1, Domgasse 5, phone 52 40 722
Tue–Sun 10 a.m.–12:15 p.m. and
1–4:30 p.m.

Austrian Museum of Applied Arts
(Österr. Museum für angewandte
Kunst)
1, Stubenring 5, phone 72 56 96
Mon, Thu–Sun 11 a.m.–6 p.m.

Museum of Fine Arts (Kunsthistorisches
Museum)
1, Maria-Theresien-Platz
(entrance)/Burgring 5 (administration),
phone 93 45 41

New Gallery in the "Stallburg",
1, Reitschulgasse 2
Mon, Wed, Thu, Sat, Sun
10 a.m.–4 p.m.

**Museum of the Cathedral and the Dio-
cese**
(Erzbischöfl. Dom- und Diözesanmuseum)
1, Stephansplatz 6, 1st floor, phone
51 5 52/598
Wed to Sat 10 a.m.–4 p.m., Sun and
holidays 10 a.m.–1 p.m.

Austrian National Library (Österr.
Nationalbibliothek) Grand Hall (Prunk-
saal)
1, Josefsplatz 1, phone 533 70 26
Mon–Sat 11 a.m.–12 noon, May to
October (exhibition)
Mon–Sat 10 a.m.–4 p.m.

National Theater (Burgtheater)
1, Dr.-Karl-Lueger-Ring 2, phone
53 24–21 80

Neidhart frescos
1, Tuchlauben 19, phone 63 80 452
Tue–Sun 10 a.m.–12:15 p.m. and
1–4:30 p.m.

Old Smithy (Alte Schmiede)
1, Schönlaterngasse 9, phone 52 83 29
Museum: Mon–Fri 9 a.m.–3 p.m.

Roman Ruins below Hoher Markt
1, Hoher Markt 3, phone 65 87 47
Tue–Sun 10 a.m.–12:15 p.m. and
1–4:30 p.m.

Spanish Riding School
1, Hofburg, Josefsplatz
Performances and training sessions: see
special folder

State Opera House (Staatsoper)
1, Opernring 2, phone 53 24–24 21

St. Stephen's Cathedral
1, Stephansplatz, phone 51 5 52/563
Guided tours of the Cathedral: Mon–
Sat 10:30 a.m. and 3 p.m., Sundays and
holidays 3 p.m. Evening guided tours:
June–September Sat 7 p.m.

Treasuries (Schatzkammer)
As of June 1987: 1, Hofburg, Schweizerhof, phone 53 36 046, Mon, Wed–Fri
10 a.m.–6 p.m., Sat, Sun 9 a.m.–6 p.m.

**Treasury of the Order of Teutonic
Knights**
(Schatzkammer des Deutschen Ordens)
1, Singerstrasse 7, phone 512 10 656
Daily 10 a.m.–12, Tue, Wed, Fri and
Sat also 3–5 p.m.

St. Virgil's Chapel
1, Stephansplatz, Underground Station
phone 52 20 503, Tue–Son
10 a.m.–12:15 p.m. and 1–4:30 p.m.